Tables & Spreads

Tables

Shelly Westerhausen Worcel

with Wyatt Worcel

&

A GO-TO GUIDE
for Beautiful Snacks, Intimate
Gatherings, and Inviting Feasts

Spreads

CHRONICLE BOOKS
SAN FRANCISCO

Library of Congress Cataloging-in-Publication Data:

Names: Worcel, Shelly Westerhausen, author,
    photographer. | Worcel, Wyatt, author.
Title: Tables & spreads : a go-to guide for beautiful
snacks, intimate gatherings, and inviting feasts / Shelly
    Westerhausen Worcel, with Wyatt Worcel.
Other titles: Tables and spreads
Description: San Francisco : Chronicle Books, [2021] |
    Includes index.
Identifiers: LCCN 2020036443 | ISBN 9781797206493
    (hardcover) | ISBN
    9781797206509 (ebook)
Subjects: LCSH: Cooking (Relishes) | Appetizers. | Table
    setting and decoration.
Classification: LCC TX740 .W44 2021 | DDC 641.81/2--dc23
    LC record available at https://lccn.loc.gov/2020036443

Manufactured in China.

Prop styling by Shelly Westerhausen Worcel.
Food styling by Shelly Westerhausen Worcel.
Design by Lizzie Vaughan.
Typesetting by Taylor Roy.

10 9 8 7 6 5 4 3 2

Chronicle books and gifts are available at special quantity
discounts to corporations, professional associations,
literacy programs, and other organizations. For details
and discount information, please contact our premiums
department at corporatesales@chroniclebooks.com or at
1-800-759-0190.

Chronicle Books LLC
680 Second Street
San Francisco, California 94107
www.chroniclebooks.com

Part 1

Building a Spread 17

Part 2

Recipes, Boards & Tables 95

Section 3

Holiday Showstoppers 202

INTRODUCTION

I was lucky to grow up in a family of both hosts and grazers. My mom remembers that it was the norm for my grandma to have a weeknight grazing table—a table filled with an array of visually striking foods that are tied together by a common theme or that work well together when served. It would be set up for when my grandpa got home from work so they could have a cocktail and snacks together before she started on dinner. I've always thought this was such a nice way to end the day and start the evening.

My mother's hosting was more casual, with pre-made dips and chips, but she would always have a small appetizer table set up when people came over. Hours in advance of the party, she would place all of the soon-to-be-filled bowls in strategic (easy-to-reach) positions on the table as reminders of what needed to be put out and where.

My father and stepmom also kept it simple with their decorating and would set up for parties on a large bar my father built in our finished basement. They'd scatter the snack bowls across it and stock the beer fridge. Done!

My stepdad went through a phase in which he loved to cook for dinner parties. He'd spend all day in the kitchen, tag-teaming with my mom, who would handle table setting and cleanup. Looking back, all these parties and food tables were completely different, but they all served the same rewarding purpose: to provide amusement, delicious food, strong drinks, and an easy excuse to gather with friends and family.

Now I'm hosting my own gatherings, which are a blend of all the above. Most often, I turn to the grazing table set up in the dining room with a spread of food and a serve-yourself drink station. It's such an easy and fuss-free way to serve guests delicious food without requiring we sit down at a particular time to eat. It also allows me to enjoy my own party by setting up the grazing table beforehand instead of scrambling to plate food for a sit-down dinner while guests are around.

In my previous cookbook, *Platters and Boards*, I shared recipes for spreads and suggested what surfaces to serve them on; with this book, I wanted to go even deeper. Here I venture beyond the board to teach you how to create and style a table just as I style tables. This is to help you end up with a visually cohesive, themed party vibe, instead of being hyper-focused on a single board.

This book focuses more on entertaining than *Platters and Boards* did, but it is still a great resource for weeknight cooking—just skip some of the styling suggestions in part 1 to create low-key weeknight combos. Entertaining and creating boards should not feel hard or intimidating, and I've created this book to help you master—or at least dabble in—both. Because who doesn't love making (and eating) food that looks great? I've given you more information than you may ever need, so you can pick and choose what excites you to put together: spreads, boards, platters, or tables that make you proud, happy—and never hungry!

Have you ever wanted to create a beautiful grazing table but have no idea where to start?

We've all seen it: that perfectly curated grazing table on Instagram or at a friend's house. Yet no matter how much time or effort you put into food prep for your party, it never looks quite as cohesive. Or maybe you saw a gorgeous spread in a magazine and said, "I can make that!" but when you tried to re-create it, it looked nothing like the picture. You followed the directions exactly, so what happened?

When you created your grazing table or spread in the past, there is a good chance the focus was on the food rather than the presentation. Maybe it's because that darn magazine provided a recipe but no notes on serving or styling the food. Or maybe

it's because you were so obsessed with that delicious dip your friend served that you didn't take a mental note of the gorgeous bouquet of flowers and matching linens that brought the table together.

How to use this book

This book will teach you not only how to make delicious, beautiful recipes, but also how to style them and design a stunning grazing table every time.

This book is split up into two parts. Part 1 is a guide to help you create stunning spreads for any occasion. It's filled with practical tips for styling both the food and the table. We will do a deep dive into all the elements that make a perfect tablescape, including how to pick the best ingredients and styling pieces, and how to put it all together to create a beautiful table every time.

You can skip around part 1 (it doesn't have to be read in order) to learn about areas of the styling process you might not be as familiar with. Use part 1 as a resource as you work through the recipes and spreads in part 2. For example, if you are making the Puppy Bowl (Super Bowl) Crudités & Dips Spread (page 212) and need some inspiration on how to pick out the perfect vegetables, look back at pages 53 to 55 for how to shop for and prep vegetables.

Part 2 is where you'll find the spread themes and recipes. If you are already a fan of my previous cookbook, *Platters and Boards*, then you will be pleased to find part 2 laid out in a similar fashion. There are twenty-one board themes with over sixty-five recipes in this section. Each theme includes styling notes, recipes, and a drink pairing suggestion. Depending on how robust you'd like your final spread to be, you can pick and choose a single recipe to prepare, or make all the recipes within a single theme.

As I did with *Platters and Boards*, I've recruited my partner, Wyatt, to provide suggested meat pairings throughout the book. I've been a vegetarian for close to twenty years, so I needed to bring in an expert to help guide those recommendations. Unless otherwise noted, you can assume all other writing in this book is coming from me (Shelly!).

I tried to cram a lot into these pages, which meant organizing this book properly was key. To ensure it's easy to follow, I've created these visual keys that you'll find throughout the book:

SPREAD TYPE

WYATT'S SIDEBAR

STYLING NOTES

MAKE-AHEAD GAME PLAN

DRINK PAIRING

NOTES

Where to go from here

If you are already a styling master and just here for the recipes, feel free to skip ahead to part 2 (page 95), where you'll find an array of theme ideas and recipes. If you'd like to learn more about creating stunning presentations and everything that entails, turn the page and let's get started with part 1: Building a Spread.

Part 1:
Building
a Spread

Section 1

The Spread

WHAT IS A SPREAD?

For the purposes of this book, a spread is a series of platters, boards, and servingware that are grouped together by a common theme to create an abundant display of food. Spreads are a great option for both entertaining a crowd and feeding a small group for several reasons:

They let you enjoy a variety of food in one sitting without having to create elaborate recipes.

They are easy to scale up and down depending on the number of people you plan to feed.

They make it easy to create a meal that feels cohesive, meaningful, and curated to your gathering.

Five Qs to Start

When planning your spread, start by asking yourself these five questions. They will help you choose a board and scale it as necessary.

 What is the event or occasion?

Some spreads are easily tied to themes and special occasions, while others are more general. Decide the purpose of your spread to help you narrow down the options. See the list of boards for occasions on pages 90 to 93.

2 How many guests will you have?

All the spreads in this book are easy to scale up and down. Get a rough head count so you'll know if you need to double, triple, or halve the spread.

 What time of year is your event taking place?

Some spreads make more sense for certain times of year based on what is in season and what the temperature is outside (the Creamy Polenta Spread [page 132] just feels like a cozy, cold-weather food, while the Time to Celebrate Paloma Party spread (page 146) is best saved for sunny days).

4 Where is the event taking place?

Is there space for a grazing table? Will it be a sit-down meal served family style, or a help-yourself-and-sit-where-you-can kind of event? Will you need to transport anything by car to another location and, if so, which elements of the spread can be made ahead?

 How much time do you have to dedicate to planning, food prep, and cooking?

Some spreads require more make-ahead prep, while others can be whipped up on the fly. Decide how much time you are willing to dedicate to preparing for the event and choose your spread accordingly.

TIMELINE FOR BUILDING A SPREAD

I've created this timeline to help all the total planners out there (like me!) who like to map everything out. You could easily whip up most of these spreads on a day's notice, but if you give yourself the time, you can really create a stunning spread without the stress of scrambling.

1 WEEK AHEAD	☐ Answer the five Qs (see page 21).
	☐ Pick out which spread(s) you are planning to tackle and decide if you'll need to double or halve anything based on your guest count.
	☐ Create a grocery list for everything you'll need.
3 DAYS BEFORE	☐ Go grocery shopping.
2 DAYS BEFORE	☐ Pick out all the servingware and the wow-factor decorations (see pages 68 to 87) for the table.
1 DAY BEFORE	☐ Prep any recipes you are planning to serve that can be made ahead.
	☐ Pick up flowers for the table arrangement(s).

MORNING OF	☐ Set up your table: Build tiers, drape linen, and consider where each dish will go. I find it helpful to lay out all my empty serving platters to visualize the final display. Place any items on the table that don't need to be plated in the kitchen, such as flowers, napkins, and guest utensils.
2 HOURS BEFORE	☐ Chop all the vegetables and transfer them to sealed containers in the refrigerator.
1 HOUR BEFORE	☐ Make any last-minute recipes that couldn't be prepared ahead of time. ☐ If serving cheese, remove it from the refrigerator and plate it on your spread.
30 MINUTES BEFORE	☐ If serving cured meat, remove it from the refrigerator and plate it on your spread.
15 MINUTES BEFORE	☐ Arrange everything else you are serving on your grazing table.
MINUTES BEFORE GUESTS ARRIVE	☐ Double-check that all the food has serving utensils. ☐ Light the candles. ☐ Start your playlist. ☐ Spritz vegetables, fruit, and herbs with water (if they are starting to look dry). ☐ Put out ice (if using) and any chilled drinks. ☐ Take a moment to admire the beautiful grazing table you just spent a week planning. (Don't skip this step!)
AS GUESTS ARRIVE	☐ Hand them a drink, mingle, and dig into your spread!

Section 2

The Basics

THE BASICS OF BUILDING A SPREAD

If you are already a proud owner of my previous cookbook, *Platters and Boards*, then some of this section may seem like a review. But these are the basic building blocks to creating a stunning spread, so we can't just skip over them! Especially since my focus in this book is on the styling aspect. Follow these easy steps to build your next spread:

1. Answer the Five Qs (page 21).

2. Find your focal point. Decide what your focal point (or North Star, as I like to call it) will be by choosing an ingredient or recipe to build your spread around. It could be a recipe from this book, a special holiday dish, or an anchor ingredient you picked up at the farmers' market. Whatever it is, keep it in mind when choosing all the other elements in the spread for a unified presentation and cohesive feeling.

3. Pick out complementary foods. Once you have that star ingredient or recipe picked out, it's time to decide what kind of food will either be enjoyed with or alongside it. For example, if you have a piece of salty hard cheese that you are obsessed with from the local cheese shop, you'll want to make sure there are plenty of simple crackers and sweet jam on the board to serve it with. I recommend trying to incorporate something salty, sweet, savory, and tangy into each spread.

4. Pick out your surface(s). Choose which boards, trays, or platters you'll use to display your food. When deciding what to use, think of the size, shape, height, and color; whether you want them to match perfectly or complement each other; and how they will look with the food you are serving. For more ideas on surfaces to use and styling tips, see page 30.

5. Start assembling your spread! In general, it's a good idea to begin setting up your board about an hour before your guests arrive (see the timeline on page 22). Start by positioning your star ingredient or recipe. If it's a large portion (like an entire wheel of cheese or a dip that serves twenty), consider splitting it up and placing it in different areas on the spread to create a fuller look and allow easier access for all of your guests.

From there, add accompaniments, one at a time, until the spread looks full (it's totally personal preference if you like to pile your board high or keep it spare—more on that in the Anatomy of a Spread section, page 88). Make sure to group items meant to be eaten together near each other. If any food you are planning to serve could spread or seep into other items, place it in its own bowl or on a separate small plate.

6. Add utensils and tools; guests shouldn't use their hands. Provide tongs or a cheese knife for each type of cheese, spoons for anything liquid or spreadable, and little forks or tongs for meat.

7. Incorporate garnishes. I recommend avoiding nonedible presentation items. Instead, focus on beautiful edible components. Edible flowers and herbs will add visual pop to your board but still look natural. Fill any gaps in your board or spread with a garnish right before serving, since it's likely to be the first element that will wilt or discolor, and you want it to stay as pretty and fresh as possible.

Common Mistakes

I'd like to believe that there is no wrong way to create a spread. Nevertheless, some spreads are more practical and straightforward than others. Here are a few common mistakes:

Getting too far off theme. It's important to remember that, at the end of the day, your spread is about eating. Don't get carried away with board components that don't mix with your North Star. These items will most likely not get eaten, and they will make your spread feel random.

Overdoing it. We've all seen that "epic" spread that is actually just a table where every inch is covered with food. It's overwhelming and distracting when there is so much *stuff* that you can no longer identify the unifying theme or ingredient, and your guests won't even know where to start! Make sure your grazing table feels approachable, inviting, and not intimidating for your guests.

Mixing board components. Boards start to look busy when you mix all your accompaniments together in one big pile (for example, tossing together carrots and bell pepper strips instead of placing them in their own individual piles next to each other). You want to be able to clearly see each component of the board—even if you prefer an abundant-looking spread.

Not timing it out. No one wants to eat cold food that is meant to be served warm and vice versa, so make sure to create your game plan ahead of time so everything is enjoyed at its ideal temperature.

Putting out too much food right away. Some food is best kept chilled rather than left out at room temperature for hours (such as cheese and meats), so consider holding back half of the food you prepped and replenishing the spread halfway through the party.

PORTIONING A SPREAD

	Starter or After Dinner	Main
CHEESE	1 to 1½ oz [30 to 40 g] per person	2 to 4 oz [55 to 115 g] per person
NUTS	1 to 2 Tbsp per person	2 to 3 Tbsp per person
CONDIMENTS	1 to 2 Tbsp per person	3 to 4 Tbsp per person
FRUIT	4 bite-size pieces per person	4 to 5 bite-size pieces per person
VEGETABLES	4 to 6 bite-size pieces per person	6 to 10 bite-size pieces per person
COOKIES	2 cookies per person	
CHIPS	1 oz [30 g] per person	
MEAT	1 to 2 oz [30 to 55 g] per person	2 to 3 oz [55 to 85 g] per person

There are two kinds of people in this world: those who underestimate everything and those who overestimate everything. I've always fallen into the overestimating category, so I started using this portioning chart to keep my expectations in line. While you don't want to run out of food an hour into your event, you also don't want to end up with a ton of leftovers when it's over. Assuming you are planning to serve a variety of goods, this chart is a great way to calculate how much food you need for your spread.

All of the spreads in this book can easily be scaled up or down to accommodate almost any number of guests. I've calculated all the yields for the spreads in this book with the above grid in mind, so use this diagram as a reference.

ESSENTIALS & ENHANCEMENTS FOR YOUR TABLE SPREAD

The key to creating a stunning presentation is to use gorgeous tableware that will complement your food. This next section is going to dive into all the different types of tableware that you can incorporate to bring your table to the next level. Of course, you don't need all of these items to throw a successful party. Pick and choose the items that appeal to you most (although I definitely recommend at least a few nice boards and platters).

Serving Dishes: Platters, Boards & Trays

Platters, boards, and trays can all be used interchangeably, and I recommend picking them out right after you decide on a theme and before you start choosing other servingware for your table.

Since the options for platters, boards, and trays are pretty endless, picking out the perfect one can feel overwhelming. Here are a few things to keep in mind when choosing your serving dishware:

Material

The most common serving dish materials are ceramic, wood, marble, or even glass, so how do you know which one to pick?

Wood surfaces are the most traditional option for a cheese board. It's fairly common, which means you'll be able to easily find different shapes and sizes at a home goods store or online (make sure you choose one with a food-safe finish). Look for nonporous wood, such as olive wood, hard maple, or birch, as it will be less likely to absorb strong flavors from the food. Clean your boards after each use with warm, soapy water and wipe dry immediately.

Marble is another lovely option. I love the clean look and the way bright colors pop against its white base (unless, of course, you are using black or colored marble, which is harder to track down but also a gorgeous option!). The dense properties of marble make it great for keeping your food cool—perfect for those hot days when you are worried about your food warming up too quickly in the sun. Marble is usually quite heavy, though, so I wouldn't recommend it if you are planning to take your food to go (such as taking it on a picnic). Another disadvantage is that it stains easily, so you'll want to avoid putting vibrant vegetables (like beets) directly on the board.

Ceramic platters are very common and come in endless color options, so you won't have any trouble finding a shade that matches your color scheme (more on that on page 77).

Additionally, most ceramic platters are dishwasher safe. (Easy cleanup? Yes please!) Because they are so readily available, you can find them at almost any price point—look for platters at your local secondhand store, or source from a home goods shop for pricier but on-point trendy options.

Glass platters have also been making a comeback lately, which I'm going to attribute to the fact that you can source them pretty cheaply from most second-hand shops. I like using glass that is either colored (to give a fantastic vintage vibe) or textured, which lends an interesting contrast to the food. Most glassware is also dishwasher safe, which makes it a great option for easy cleanup.

Additional material options to consider include plastic (which I normally find looks a little too informal for most of the gatherings I'm hosting), slate, and even pink salt slabs!

Shape

Choosing the shape of your serving dish is all personal preference. (Not very helpful, I know. You are going to have to make this decision yourself!) The most common shapes you'll come across are oval, round, rectangular, and square. I like to mix and match shapes for contrast, but again, there is no right answer!

You'll also need to decide if you'd like your serving dish to be rimmed or flat. If you need to move your serving dish for any reason throughout the night (such as if you're passing it around a table) then you'll want a rimmed dish. Flat options, like wood or marble cheese board plates, are great for grazing tables where you can leave it in one place all night long.

Mix & Match

It generally looks more formal to use a unified set of plates and utensils, while mixing and matching can come across as playful and uniquely you. A hodgepodge of dishware also adds more personality and means you don't have to go out and buy four sets of everything just to match. Just make sure you stay on a certain theme so it doesn't feel too random—pick plates in the same color palette or size, glasses with similar shapes, and so on.

Size

While there is a lot of creative decision-making when it comes to choosing the material and shape, the size of your serving dish is all about practicality. In general, you should choose a size that is large enough to accommodate an entire dish without leaving a lot of excess space that will make it look lacking. If you don't have a large enough platter or your table isn't big enough to accommodate one big dish, you have two options: Either use several dishware pieces and group them together on the table to make a spread, or put out a smaller portion to start and refill as needed.

Also consider whether you want to create an abundance spread or a statement piece (see page 93). If you want to have some space between the food, pick out a larger board that provides the food with room to breathe; if you prefer the abundant look, go with a small- to medium-size board so you can pile it high with food without it starting to look too overwhelming.

Small Bowls & Plates

Small bowls and plates are crucial for keeping certain foods from seeping into and potentially ruining other food on the tray. I recommend investing in an array of bowls that are 2 oz [60 ml] and smaller, and plates that are 3 in [7.5 cm] and smaller. The small bowls can be used for liquids and spreadables like honey, jams, dips, some fresh cheeses, and olives with their juices. Small plates will be perfect for strong cheeses that you don't want to mix with other foods, as well as chopped herbs that can quickly get messy.

Layering with small dishes and bowls is one of my favorite tricks to keep a board visually interesting. If you're using a flat surface, I like to have some of the smaller bowls hang off the board slightly to give the feeling of the board overflowing with goodies (without actually pushing food off the board). Make sure you fill up the bowl or plate so it doesn't look skimpy or lacking.

Serving Utensils & Party Picks

I won't be able to cover ALL the serving utensil options out there–that could be an entire book on its own! Instead, I'll focus on ones that will be most practical for the spreads in this book.

In general, you'll want to make sure that you have utensils that your guests can use to serve themselves, and utensils they can use to eat (silverware). It's worth noting that you will most likely want to invest in some nice serving spoons, tongs, ladles, and silverware.

When thinking about utensils, the first step is to figure out what kind of food you will be serving. If you are mostly serving traditional grazing fare in the form of finger food, offer party picks. These could be as simple as toothpicks or as fancy as handmade party picks with washi tape (see the panel on page 34 for a DIY!). Either way, plan to have around three to five party picks per guest, or five to seven if you have a lot of a food or the party will last more than four hours. You can usually buy them in bulk pretty cheaply, and many party stores have an array of themed options. Place the party picks in a small bowl near the napkins and small plates.

Cheese Knives & Labels

I grouped cheese knives and labels together because they are both items that you'll want to include on your spread *if* you are serving cheese.

Make sure to place each cheese knife on or near the cheese it accompanies so guests know which variety it should be used with. If I'm serving a wheel of cheese, I usually use the knife to cut it open and have a few slices already portioned out so it feels more inviting for the guests to dive right in. For soft cheeses, I put the knife right into the bowl with the cheese, and for hard cheeses, I usually stick it right in the top of the wedge.

Each cheese should have its own knife to avoid mixing flavors. Most cheese knife sets come with several different-shaped knives, which are meant for different cheeses. Here is a quick summary of some of the most common cheese knives (if some of these terms don't make sense to you just yet, check the cheese section on page 45 to see what kind of cheeses fall into these categories):

Cheese Knives

	FORK-TIPPED SPEAR OR PRONGED CHEESE KNIFE	Perfect for cutting soft, semisoft, and hard cheeses. The pronged tip can be used to pick up cheese slices.
	SPADE	Its sharp edge makes it ideal for cutting into hard cheeses.
	CHEESE FORK	Great for hard cheeses or blue cheeses, and ideal for transferring cheeses from the spread to your guests' plates.
	FLAT CHEESE KNIFE	Great all-purpose knife that works for everything from cutting crumbly, soft cheeses to shavings and chipping at hard cheeses.
	CHISEL KNIFE	This wide cheese knife works wonders at cutting hard, crumbly cheeses into chunks.
	SOFT CHEESE KNIFE	Use on soft cheeses and for accompanying items like jams and sauces.
	ALMOND KNIFE OR CHEESE SPREADER	Great all-purpose knife that can be used to open wheels, divide wedges, and cut through hard cheese rinds.

DIY Party Picks

Have your heart set on a theme but can't find any party picks to match it?
Here are two easy DIYs to make your own!

Option 1
Washi Tape Party Pick Flags

EQUIPMENT

Washi tape, toothpicks, scissors

PROCESS

Cut out 4 in [10 cm] pieces of washi tape and place the tape down horizontally so the sticky side is facing up. Place the top portion of the toothpick into the center of the sticky side of the washi tape so the top of the toothpick doesn't peek over the top of the tape. Fold the washi tape in half so that the sticky sides stick together and the toothpick and tape create an upside-down *L*. Use scissors to cut a sideways *V* out of the end of the washi tape to create a flag shape. Repeat the process with the washi tape and toothpicks until you have enough party picks to suit your needs.

Option 2
Themed Party Picks

EQUIPMENT

Fun-shaped hole punch (like a star or heart), thick scrapbook paper, toothpicks, hot glue gun

PROCESS

Use the hole punch to punch out an even number of shapes from the thick scrapbook paper. Place a small dab of hot glue on the back side of the bottom of a shape and then place the top of the toothpick on the hot glue. Place the reverse side of another shape on top so the two shapes line up and the toothpick is wedged between the two shapes. Repeat with the rest of the shapes and toothpicks.

Another great tool for serving cheese is cheese labels. They make it easy for you to call out the different kinds you are serving so you don't have to spend all night telling people what is what. Labels also allow your guests to make mental notes if they end up liking a cheese they've never had before and want to buy it in the future. I personally love to throw a few unique cheeses onto my cheese boards (while always keeping a few favorites so people aren't too thrown off), and labeling them allows my guests to see that I put extra effort into curating the spread for them. If you'd like to go above and beyond, you could even add a few key words to let your guests know more about the cheese (such as the country of origin, milk it's made from, flavor profile, etc.).

Additional Useful Utensils

A few other utensils that will come up throughout this book:

Ladle: If you've ever made homemade soup before, you probably already have one of these on hand, but if you're creating a spread that involves a main course served in bowls, you'll probably want to have some type of ladle available. A few boards from this book this might be handy for: Fall Oatmeal Spread (page 106), Creamy Polenta Spread (page 132), and Mother's Day Spring Minestrone Soup Spread (page 230).

Salad Servers & Tongs: Anytime you are incorporating a lot of greens into your spread, it is probably time to pull out the salad tongs. You can find anything from the old-style scissor salad tongs to flashy servers made out of marble.

Small serving tongs are also great to use when serving cubed cheeses to help your guests grab a single piece without touching the whole pile.

Serving Spoons & Forks: I can't think of one spread in this book that doesn't require several serving spoons or forks to help guests get items from the spread to their plates. If you are creating a finger-foods type of spread, then you may be able to rely on guests using party picks to grab their food; otherwise, a spoon or fork will be needed. For smaller-portioned items like garnishes, jams, and sauces, you'll want to use small spoons that both look proportionate to the item being served and keep guests from serving themselves too much. It's the same idea for large portions served in big salad bowls or serving plates: Use a larger spoon or fork that looks proportionate to the bowl.

Stir Sticks: If you are serving a drink spread, you may want to have stirrers on hand for your guests. Stirrers come in a variety of sizes, shapes, and materials to fit any type of party. If you host often, I recommend investing in some nice glass stirrers, but if gatherings are less frequent for you, disposable bamboo or plastic ones should work just fine. A few boards from this book stirrers might be handy for: New Year's Eve Martini Bar (page 276), Boozy Bloody Mary Bar (page 192), School's Out Summer Limeade Party (page 238), and Time to Celebrate Paloma Party (page 146).

Glassware

Glassware is another topic that can quickly feel overwhelming because there are so many different shapes and types of glasses out there. The two categories of glassware are *stemware* (drinking glasses with long stems, such as wineglasses and Champagne flutes) and *barware* (drinking glasses with solid, flat bases). Luckily for us, glasses are oftentimes named after what should be served in them. I'm going to dive into the most common ones below, but remember that you won't need ALL of these for every event. You will most certainly need different glassware for a bachelorette party (hiii shot glasses!) than a backyard barbecue (looking at you, beer glasses).

When shopping for glassware, seek out quality glass that isn't so thin that it will break easily. I look for unique features like carved patterns and unusual glass shapes to bring extra texture to the drink's appearance. I also love to check out secondhand stores to find affordable vintage options. Depending on the style of your tablescape, you could even mix and match vintage glasses if you are unable to find enough of the same set.

If you are hosting a casual get-together, then there is a charm to using the mismatched glassware you have in your kitchen cabinet. For gatherings that don't have a formal sit-down table set, I will put out the mismatched glassware on the drink table for guests to grab as needed.

Water Glasses

Water glasses are going to be essential no matter what type of gathering you are hosting. If it's a formal sit-down event, I recommend using uniform glasses that match your tablescape. If you have tall candles and

flowers, consider using taller 18 oz [530 ml] glasses to match. If your tablescape doesn't have a ton of height, keep it simple with 12 oz [360 ml] glasses. It's also worth noting that water glasses can be great all-purpose glasses for informal events if you don't want to coordinate a different glass for every drink you are serving.

Wineglasses

If you're serving a cheese board or simple appetizers for happy hour, wine might be the only beverage you need. Some people may lead you to believe that you need a different wineglass for each type of wine, but I personally believe keeping it simple is key here. Wine should be enjoyable and easy to serve, not something intimidating and elite. At the end of the day, most of your guests (myself included!) won't be terribly fussy, and your wine is going to taste close to the same out of whatever glass shape you serve it in (if you are planning to host a group of sommeliers, that may be a different story). So save your money by purchasing a few simple, all-purpose wineglasses and use that extra dough to splurge on a nicer bottle of wine. And guess what? The average wine drinker (which is most of us!) will likely be paying more attention to the flavor of the wine than the shape of the wineglass.

So what does an all-purpose, "universal" wineglass look like? You'll want to look for a clear and thin glass, usually with a stem, that has a bowl that's larger than the top of the glass. Smaller wineglasses tend to be associated with white wine, while big ones go more with red, so it makes sense that you are looking for a middle-of-the-road compromise with this one. You'll often find this classified as a Bordeaux wineglass when shopping for glassware.

Glass Guide

Water

18 OZ [530 ML]   12 OZ [360 ML]

Wine

FLUTE   RED WINE   STEMLESS

UNIVERSAL   WHITE WINE

Beer

MUG | IMPERIAL | IPA | PILSNER

PINT | RASTAL TEKU | STOUT | TULIP

Cocktail

COUPE | HIGHBALL | LOWBALL | SHOT

If you do have a palette for wine and would like to use special glasses, purchasing wineglasses made specifically for red, white, and sparkling wines is an option. Larger glasses help full-bodied red wines circulate, and using stemmed glasses for whites will keep your hand from heating up the wine. Champagne flutes, with their iconic shape, can be great for celebratory events. Sparkling wines (such as Cava, Prosecco, etc.) can be served in white wineglasses.

Another option for wines is to use stemless wineglasses. These tend to be associated with a "modern feel" and are ideal for less formal events like picnics because their sturdy bodies tend to travel well. They are also really great for everyday use, as many people find them simpler to clean (with no stem to break) and easier to fit into your cabinets. A drawback of the stemless glass, though, is that your hand on the glass could warm a chilled wine too quickly.

Beer Glasses

There are dozens of options when matching beer glasses to the type of beer you are serving. I recommend sticking with the American pint glass, which is a great all-purpose 16 oz [480 ml] beer glass that is slightly wider at the mouth than at the base.

If you want to get creative with your beer glasses, you could also consider using beer mugs, imperial pint glasses (which can hold 20 oz [600 ml] and are often used for British ales and lagers like pale ale and amber ale), pilsner glasses (for pilsners), tulip glasses (for Belgian ales), IPA glasses, stout glasses, or Teku stemmed glasses (for sours).

Beer tends to be served in more casual and laid-back settings, so if you're hosting a casual gathering, feel free to treat beer glasses like you would water glasses and leave out a variety of whatever glasses you have on hand so guests can pick which one to use. Let's be honest—most of your beer-drinking friends probably won't even pour their beers out of the bottle, so I wouldn't overthink this type of glass too much (or is that just my friends?).

If possible, I recommend getting glass versions of whatever drinkware you plan to use, as glass will look and feel the classiest. If you don't own enough glassware, you could consider renting them for your event—look for places that usually rent for weddings or corporate parties to find a large selection.

If glass is not an option, you can purchase plastic cups to use instead, particularly if you are having a less formal gathering, planning to serve near a pool, or think that some guests could potentially get a little sloppy (again—only my friends?). I always pull out the plastic glassware for events like birthday parties and grill outs.

Cocktail Glasses: Highball, Coupe, Shot Glasses, Martini, Etc.

As with beer and wineglasses, there are dozens of different types of cocktail glasses out there for pretty much any kind of cocktail you can think of. Here are a few of the most common and my personal favorites:

If only picking out one glass for mixed drinks, make it a 12 oz [360 ml] highball glass. Highball glasses are tall and chimney shaped, and are ideal for gin and tonics, vodka sodas, and Bloody Marys. Most mixed drinks can be served in this glass, and 12 oz [360 ml] is a great all-purpose size.

For serving spirits neat or on the rocks and for classic cocktails, you'll want to invest in single and double rocks glasses (also called lowballs). These are short tumblers with a solid base and usually come in 6 to 8 oz [180 to 240 ml] (single) and 8 to 10 oz [240 to 300 ml] (double) sizes. Use a single glass for serving a single spirit and double when serving classic cocktails—both should leave plenty of room to add a large chunk of ice. Common single rocks glass drinks include a neat pour of whiskey, an old-fashioned, a White Russian, and a Negroni.

A little bit more left of center than the other two glasses but one of my favorites, the coupe glass is a stemmed glass featuring a broad, shallow bowl. In recent years, it's gained popularity because of the craft cocktail movement. Although it was originally used for Champagne, it's now become a common glass for cocktails that are shaken or stirred until chilled and then served without ice (also known as "up" drinks) because the stem prevents your hands from warming the drink too quickly. It is now oftentimes the go-to selection for martinis (bye bye martini glasses!) and gimlets. The standard size is usually around 6 oz [180 ml] but look for 7 oz [210 ml] or 8 oz [240 ml] glasses if you'd like a little space between the drink and the rim, to prevent spilling.

Planning to use plastic cups at your casual gathering?

Use a permanent marker to write the names of famous people (and even animals) onto the cups! This not only lets your guests find their cup without issue, but it's also a fun conversation starter. I don't know about you, but I sure don't mind going a full evening being called Chrissy Teigen or Britney Spears.

Dinnerware for Guests

For events that require mingling, you'll want to have a way for guests to transport their food. Depending on the food you are serving and how messy it is, appetizer napkins may work just fine. If you have a more robust spread (including any sort of dip), you'll need small appetizer plates. Look for plates between 4 and 9 in [10 and 23 cm] so your guests have plenty of surface area but aren't carrying around full-size plates all night.

When possible, opt for plates made out of ceramic or glass; they will look and feel classier. If you are serving a large and informal crowd (or children), plain white (or elegantly themed) paper plates will also work. Appetizer plates will work for 90 percent of gatherings, but if you are serving something liquid, set out small bowls, teacups, or shot glasses as well. Just as with the plates, ceramic, porcelain, or glass is going to look the nicest here, but plastic or paper will work for less formal or outdoor gatherings.

If you are serving something more robust that requires cutlery, you have two options: You can pull out your fancy or everyday silverware, or you can pick up bamboo or plastic serving utensils (this will save your dishwasher but may not always be the best for the environment). If using traditional silverware, consider investing in a nice black or gold set to give an extra-special touch to the table. For disposable options, look for utensils that match your color scheme.

Remember!

Set aside space for napkins, plates, and utensils before setting up your table so you don't have to reorganize everything at the last minute or squeeze them in.

BEAUTIFUL & DELICIOUS: PREPPING, SERVING & STYLING FOOD

If, in your prep, you start to feel over-whelmed, refocus yourself on the menu and the food. At the end of the day, you are inviting guests to enjoy a meal, so make sure the food is your top priority.

Here are some simple tips to ensure good eats: Seek out the freshest ingredients (which are usually the most flavorful). This means going to your local farmers' market and specialty stores—sources that are passionate about the food. Use these vendors as resources. Ask them what is in season, what would pair well together, and how best to serve an ingredient.

It's important to keep your ingredients as fresh as possible after purchase by storing them properly. I provide notes on how to store specific ingredients in the following sections, but you should always feel empowered to ask your butcher, the farmer at the market stand, or the clerk at the specialty store if you are unsure how to properly store an ingredient.

Here we'll cover some of the most common ingredients found in spreads and ways to prep, store, and style them. To start, let's talk about balancing flavors and textures.

Balancing Flavors & Textures

As with any well-seasoned dish, when deciding which foods to include in your spread, you'll want to offer a range of flavors and textures to keep the board interesting. This allows your guests to mix and match to create a satisfying array of samplings. I like to think of foods in the following flavor groups for spreads (there are more, but these are the ones I always try to have represented): savory, salty, tangy, and sweet.

It is also a good idea to feature a variety of textures in your spread. For example, serve some crusty bread with a soup spread, or include some crunchy pickled vegetables next to gooey Brie and crackers.

Keep these categories in mind when building your spreads. If your board feels lacking, see if it's missing one of these categories. To expand your board even more, consider adding in something bitter, sour, or spicy (such as cajun-spiced nuts, or olives with lemon zest) to hit on even more flavor profiles.

FLAVOR PROFILES

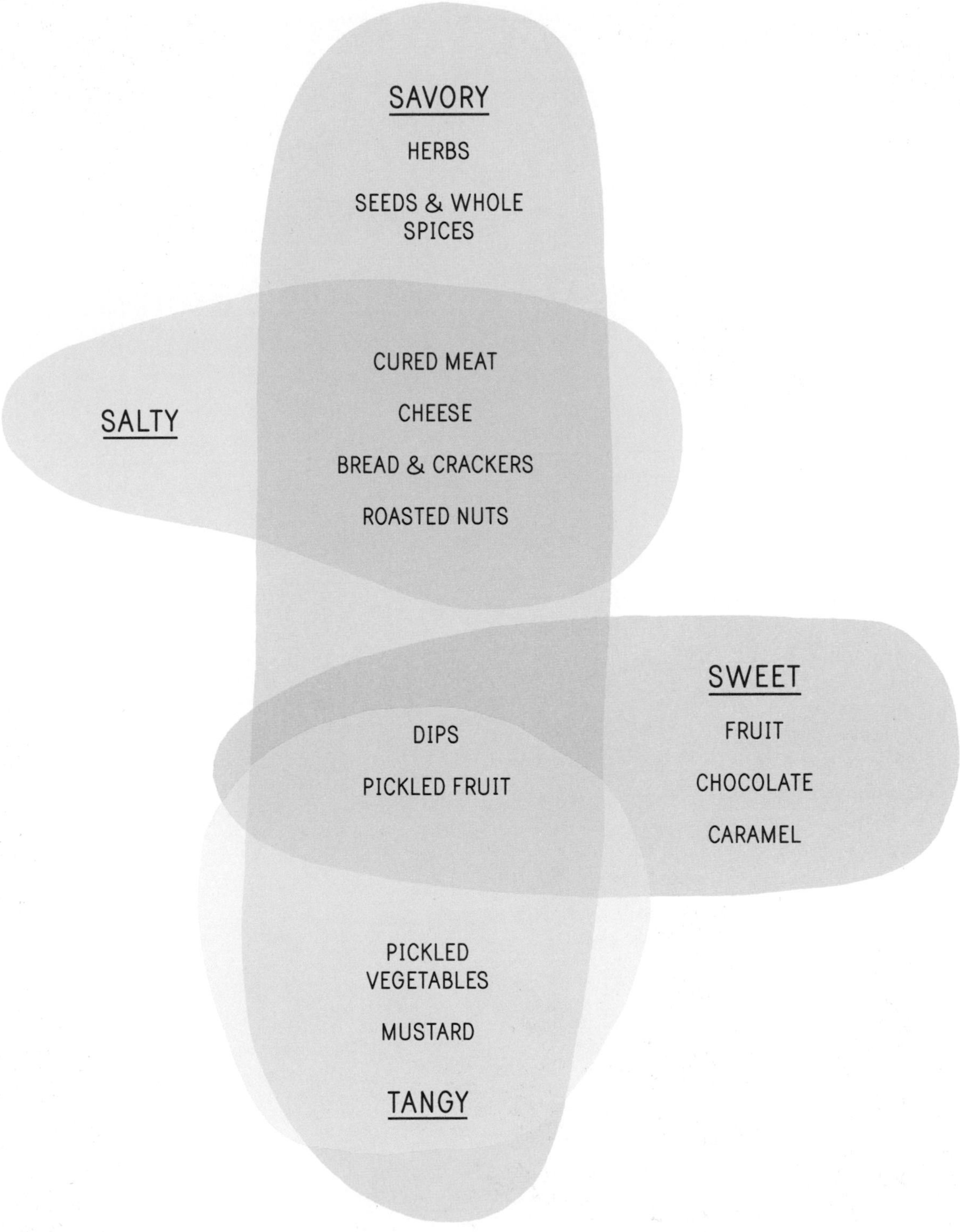

SAVORY

HERBS

SEEDS & WHOLE
SPICES

SALTY

CURED MEAT

CHEESE

BREAD & CRACKERS

ROASTED NUTS

SWEET

FRUIT

CHOCOLATE

CARAMEL

DIPS

PICKLED FRUIT

PICKLED
VEGETABLES

MUSTARD

TANGY

Cheese

No spread is more iconic than the cheese board, so it just makes sense to start here. There are several ways to categorize cheese: by type of milk, ripening process, country of origin, texture (hard or soft), or age, to name a few. I tend to focus on texture and flavor. Here is how I prefer to group cheeses:

Fresh cheese is often called *unripened* because it has not been pressed or aged. It's spreadable and soft with a creamy texture and mild flavor. By using different types of milk, varying amounts of salt, and different amounts of moisture, this category creates a range of uniquely different but mild flavors to complement a large variety of foods. These cheeses are perfect for adding a simple touch; most fresh cheese can be topped with a drizzle of quality olive oil and fresh herbs, or a drizzle of honey, to create an easy and delicious (sweet or salty!) addition to your spread. Creamy feta, ricotta, cream cheese, cottage cheese, burrata, mozzarella, and mascarpone are all fresh cheeses.

Soft-ripened cheese tends to have creamy, earthy insides with a thin white rind of blooming mold. Since these cheeses ripen from the outside in, the inside is usually runny. These cheeses are perfect for enjoying on a cracker with some jam or honey. Examples include Brie and Camembert.

Semisoft cheese usually has a relatively short aging period, which results in a moist and creamy cheese. Most are firm but not too hard, and usually pliable enough to bend slightly. Examples include fontina, provolone, Havarti, and Jarlsberg.

Blue cheese is best known for its striking characteristic of having spidery blue mold veins and a pungent flavor and frangrance. Most cheeses age from the outside in, but for this cheese to turn blue, the cheese is pierced so mold can mature inside the air patches and develop the cheese's distinct flavor. The unique color, flavor, and appearance of blue cheese make it a great choice for spreads, paired with apple slices, honey, baguette, or spicy nuts. Examples include Gorgonzola, Roquefort, and Stilton.

Semihard cheese is the largest category of cheeses on the market. The length of the aging process, which is typically anywhere between one and six months, determines the hardness and distinct sharpness of flavor, and yields a firm but slightly springy texture. These cheeses are perfect for melting onto grilled cheeses or eating in bite-size pieces as a snack. Examples include Cheddar, Gouda, Monterey Jack, Gruyère, and Swiss.

Cheese Cuts

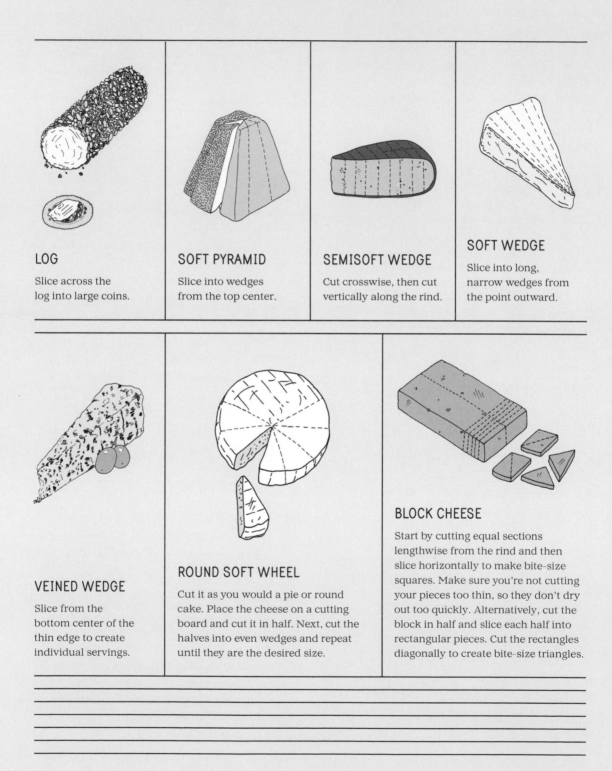

LOG

Slice across the log into large coins.

SOFT PYRAMID

Slice into wedges from the top center.

SEMISOFT WEDGE

Cut crosswise, then cut vertically along the rind.

SOFT WEDGE

Slice into long, narrow wedges from the point outward.

VEINED WEDGE

Slice from the bottom center of the thin edge to create individual servings.

ROUND SOFT WHEEL

Cut it as you would a pie or round cake. Place the cheese on a cutting board and cut it in half. Next, cut the halves into even wedges and repeat until they are the desired size.

BLOCK CHEESE

Start by cutting equal sections lengthwise from the rind and then slice horizontally to make bite-size squares. Make sure you're not cutting your pieces too thin, so they don't dry out too quickly. Alternatively, cut the block in half and slice each half into rectangular pieces. Cut the rectangles diagonally to create bite-size triangles.

Hard cheese is known for its rich umami flavor and punchy saltiness. Hard cheeses are extremely low-moisture cheeses that are oftentimes grated over dishes instead of sliced; because of this, they're less common on spreads. If you are planning to use this kind of cheese in your spread, consider grating or slicing it beforehand so guests aren't struggling at the grazing table to chip off a piece. This pairs beautifully with sweet options like dried fruit or jam. Examples include Parmesan and Manchego.

When purchasing cheese for your board, try to stick to between two and five varieties so your guests aren't overwhelmed by options. Keep it interesting by choosing a few from each of the aforementioned categories and mix both familiar cheeses (for the picky eaters) and less common varieties (to offer new discoveries to your adventurous eaters).

Prepping & Serving

Due to how cheese is ripened, each individual cheese usually contains several different layers of flavor. Make sure you are cutting it in a way that allows guests to enjoy all the layers in one bite. You should encourage guests to enjoy the rind (unless you have one that's too hard, like Parmesan rind—save that for soup!). The rind has a unique flavor that often adds to the overall flavor profile of the cheese.

As a general rule, most cheeses should be taken out of the fridge up to an hour before serving so they can warm up to room temperature. Cheese reaches its optimal flavor and texture at room temperature, and some of the more complex flavors won't shine through if it's too cold. Cheese should only be out for up to 4 hours, so if you plan to have your gathering last longer than that, set out some at the beginning of the party and bring out another round halfway through.

Styling

Select different types of cheeses and cut them in various shapes to lend variety and visual interest to your spread. Make sure none of your cheeses are touching to keep their flavors from mingling. If you're making a cheese board, place the cheeses in different areas of the board before any other components are added, and then fill in the empty space with additional items, such as crackers and nuts. If serving a semisoft or semihard cheese that won't melt, feel free to stack the slices high on the board for an abundant look. For all other cheeses, keep them lined up in one layer to avoid the pieces getting stuck together. Cut some of the cheese while keeping other parts whole so your guests know how to cut future pieces. Make sure you include a cutting or serving utensil for each kind of cheese.

Storing

- Remove any plastic wrapping, which prevents the cheese from breathing and can cause moisture build-up, discoloration, and off flavors and odors.

- Store cheese loosely wrapped in wax paper, aluminum foil, beeswax wraps, or specialty cheese paper. These will let the cheese breathe and keep it from drying out, which will help preserve its flavor.

- Transfer the wrapped cheese to an airtight container to keep the moisture level consistent and the cheese odor contained. If your refrigerator has drawers that allow temperature adjustment, store it between 40°F and 45°F [4°C and 7°C].

- Most cheeses should last for a week or two in these conditions, but they will start to lose their flavor eventually, so serve them sooner rather than later.

Meat

To keep things simple, the meat we cover in this section is going to be the kind of meat you'll find on a cheeseboard or charcuterie spread; in other words, meats that are cooked and preserved in a way that will allow them to sit out for a few hours with a lower risk of making your guests sick. Preserved with salt and/or heat to prolong shelf life and enhance flavor, most are smoked or cured and many are coated in fat to help maximize their stability and prevent spoilage. Here are two categories based on common preparation styles:

Forcemeats are a combination of lean meats that are ground, sieved, or puréed and then emulsified with fat. The most common are cured meats and pâté. Cured meats are encased in a casing tube for cooking, such as salami, sopressata, chorizo, and pepperoni. Pâté and terrine can be made out of many different kinds of meat such as duck, goose, chicken, or salmon.

Salt-cured meats use salt for preservation. This is done by drawing out and replacing the water in the meat with salt, preventing spoilage. Salt-cured meats include prosciutto, bacon, and speck.

Types of Meat

FORCEMEATS	
Cured Meats	**Pâté**
Salami	Duck
Sopressata	Goose
Chorizo	Chicken
Pepperoni	Salmon

SALT-CURED
Prosciutto
Bacon
Speck

Prepping & Serving

Cured meats come in many different flavors, and there is an optimal way to slice them to achieve the perfect flavor. Although the thickness of the slice will vary depending on how pungent the flavor is, you can generally cut the cured meat into rounds.

- For whole-muscle cuts (like proscuitto), the butcher will most likely slice these into thin pieces (make sure to tell them you'll be using this for a charcuterie board rather than sandwiches, which will affect the thickness).

- Pâté usually comes in a loaf form, so you'll want to slice it into bite-size pieces for your guests.

- If you're serving with alcohol, pair similar characteristics together. For example, match delicate meats like prosciutto or a lovely terrine with crisp white wines, light-bodied red wines, or light beer; for strong-flavored meats, such as soppressata or chorizo, pair with full-bodied reds or strong beer.

- Meat should be put out 30 minutes before guests arrive so it has time to come to room temperature. Don't keep meat out at room temperature for more than 2 hours. If it starts to look or smell off, discard it.

- Plan to put out some meat before your guests arrive and replenish the table after an hour or so.

Styling

Serving a variety of meat with different cuts will create a visually striking spread. Keep space between each type of meat so the flavors don't intermingle. For thinly sliced meats, you can lay them flat so they partially overlap like shingles, wrap them up into cylinders, fold them twice to create triangles, or delicately create mounds to add height to your spread. Round cured meat slices are a little less versatile and will look best if they are lined up in an overlapping row. For pâté, slice off a few pieces to let guests know how to serve themselves, but keep some of it whole to show off its shape.

Storing

Buy your meat within 3 to 5 days of when you plan to serve it. Keep forcemeats whole; cut salt-cured meats and wrap them in deli paper or plastic wrap. Store in the refrigerator.

Styling Meat

ROLLED UP IN CYLINDERS

Good for: Thinly sliced meat

LAID FLAT OVERLAPPED LIKE SHINGLES

Good for: Thinly sliced meat

FOLDED TWICE TO CREATE A TRIANGLE

Good for: Thinly sliced meat

SET IN MOUNDS TO CREATE HEIGHT

Good for: Thinly sliced meat

LINED UP IN AN OVERLAPPING ROW

Good for: Thick, round cured meats

SERVED WHOLE & SLICED

Good for: Pâté

Vegetables

Vegetables are my (not-so) secret weapon when it comes to creating spreads. They are versatile and come in so many colors and shapes that they always look great stacked on a platter. They are also inexpensive compared to cheese and meat, so you can stock up on them without breaking the bank. The key to making a next-level spread is to play to vegetables' strengths by serving them fresh and in abundance!

Prepping & Serving

Raw: If time allows, wait to wash and cut your vegetables until just before serving to avoid them drying out. If you do need to cut the vegetables ahead of time, wrap them in a damp cloth and store them in the refrigerator. If you are planning to display your vegetables for a short time, you may want to serve them over ice. This creates a stunning presentation, but you'll need to check on them frequently to refresh the ice and remove any water.

Cooked: Some vegetables, such as new potatoes and sweet potatoes, will need to be cooked if they are served on a crudites platter. Others can be served raw but may benefit from a quick cooking process, such as blanching, to add salt and give an extra pop of color; examples are green beans, asparagus, and broccoli. If blanching, make sure you have an ice bath at the ready so you can immediately submerge the cooked vegetables. This will help avoid overcooking and enhance the bright colors of the vegetables. I also like to blanch a vegetable if it has become slightly droopy and no longer looks its best, as salted water will help hydrate the vegetable, give it extra flavor (from the salt), and bring out the color. Cooked vegetables can be served the same way you would serve raw ones: piled high on a platter or served over ice.

Pickled: Pickled vegetables add a tangy, acidic punch to spreads and work as great palette cleansers between cheese samplings. As with raw and cooked vegetables, make sure the pickled vegetables you set out are bite size. If you can, serve them in their juices to keep them from drying out. You can find almost any vegetable in pickle form, but some of my favorites include asparagus, beets, and green beans.

Styling

A large part of creating a beautiful presentation with vegetables is making sure you are using a variety of fresh and in-season options. This will guarantee an array of vibrant colors and shapes.

- My favorite way to arrange vegetables is to pile them high in little mounds according to type. This will help each vegetable stand out and keep the presentation from feeling overwhelming; I recommend against mixing them all together like you would a salad.

- Space out similarly colored vegetables so they aren't visually blending together. For example, place green beans and green bell peppers on opposite sides of the platter and have something like purple beets or pink radishes between them.

- Do the same thing with shapes: If your carrots are cut into large matchsticks, add some round radishes or cherry tomatoes next to them.

- You can also create variety within the vegetables themselves; for example, leave some of your cherry tomatoes whole and mix in a few halves and quarters.

- If you are putting some items in bowls (like pickled vegetables) and keeping others on a platter or board, fill the space between the bowls with vegetables.

- Allow some of the vegetables to hang off the board or platter slightly (but not so much that they touch the table) to create a more organic and abundant feel.

Storing

Most vegetables can be stored in the refrigerator in a resealable container with a damp paper towel (to retain moisture). They will most likely dry out within a few days but will still be fine to eat. They can be rehydrated slightly by running them under cold water or spritzing them with water. If you have leftover whole tomatoes, keep those on the counter, as the refrigerator will alter their texture.

Vegetable Cuts

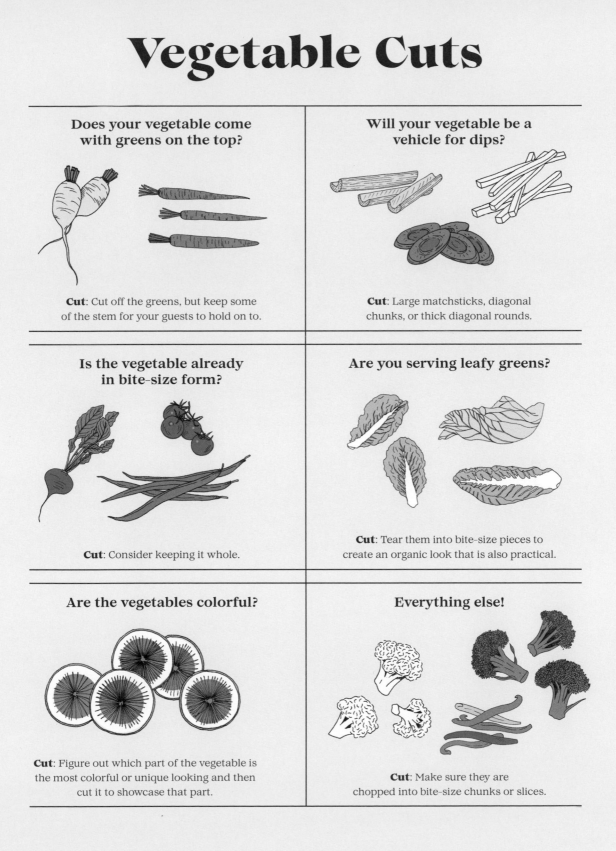

Does your vegetable come with greens on the top?

Cut: Cut off the greens, but keep some of the stem for your guests to hold on to.

Will your vegetable be a vehicle for dips?

Cut: Large matchsticks, diagonal chunks, or thick diagonal rounds.

Is the vegetable already in bite-size form?

Cut: Consider keeping it whole.

Are you serving leafy greens?

Cut: Tear them into bite-size pieces to create an organic look that is also practical.

Are the vegetables colorful?

Cut: Figure out which part of the vegetable is the most colorful or unique looking and then cut it to showcase that part.

Everything else!

Cut: Make sure they are chopped into bite-size chunks or slices.

Fresh & Dried Fruit

Fresh or dried fruit can be a great way to add a natural sweetness to your spreads that pairs beautifully with anything from sharp to creamy cheeses and salty meats. They also add a pop of color and texture since they come in such a wide variety, just like vegetables.

Prepping & Serving

Fruit comes in all different shapes and sizes, so there is not one universal way to prep and serve it, but here are a few things to keep in mind when serving fruit:

- If slicing apples, rub the slices with lemon juice to slow down the oxidation process and prevent them from turning brown. Also, make sure you think about the other items you are serving when deciding what kind of apple to include. Do you want a sour apple, like a Granny Smith, to complement sweet jam and savory cheese? Or a crisp, sweet apple, like a Fuji, to dip into a tangy dressing?

- Transfer juicy fruits to bowls to keep them away from other items on the platter. Examples include raspberries and cut pineapple. If your fruit is extra juicy (think mango or melon pieces), put toothpicks nearby so guests don't get their hands sticky when serving themselves.

- Leave berries whole when serving to keep them fresh longer.

- Like vegetables, make sure the fruit is in bite-size pieces when serving so guests don't have to worry about cutting anything themselves.

Styling

Style fruit the same way you would vegetables—by picking out a variety of fresh and in-season fruits to add to your spread. Here are a few suggestions to get you started:

- Pile the fruit into little mounds, grouped by type.

- Don't mix all the fruit together, as it'll look too busy on a large spread.

- If the inside of the fruit has a beautiful hue or interesting texture, cut the fruit to show these characteristics when serving (examples include figs, blood oranges, and Pink Lady apples).

FRUIT STORAGE

FRIDGE

BLUEBERRIES

CHERRIES

GRAPES

RASPBERRIES

STRAWBERRIES

ROOM TEMP UNTIL RIPE

APRICOTS

MANGOES

NECTARINES

PEACHES

PEARS

ROOM TEMP

BANANAS

GRAPEFRUIT

LEMONS

LIMES

ORANGES

WATERMELON

Storing

If your fresh fruit has a thick outer layer (such as bananas, watermelons, and oranges), then you'll want to keep them whole on your counter until ready to enjoy. Stone fruit can be left on the counter until ripened and then should be moved to the refrigerator. All berries should be stored in the refrigerator in a breathable container or on a damp cloth, and should not be washed until you're ready to use them. Berries tend to spoil quickly, so try to purchase them as close as possible to the date you'll be eating them. The diagram on this page shows how to store a few common fruits.

Dried fruit should be stored in a container in a cool, dry, and ideally dark place (such as the back of a cabinet). Most dried fruits can be stored this way for up to 6 months. You can also transfer dried fruit to a freezer bag and store it in the freezer for longer.

Looking to jazz up your dried fruit a bit?

Give it a quick pickle! In a small saucepan over medium heat, combine ½ cup [75 g] dried fruit (chopped apricots, yellow raisins, and figs all work well) with 2 Tbsp each of brown sugar and vinegar. Bring to a medium simmer and then remove from the heat and stir. Let sit for 15 minutes before serving. I like to serve pickled fruits in a small bowl with their juices to continue the pickling process, but you can remove the liquid at any time. These are delicious over ricotta with a little olive oil and black pepper, or sprinkled on top of a salad. Play around with different types of vinegars—I love how mild rice vinegar is, but apple cider and white wine vinegars would work great here too!

Dips, Sauces & Jams

If you've already scanned through the recipes portion of this book, then you know I've included a ton of recipes for dips, sauces, and jams. This is because they bring a creamy addition to your boards and can fill out any flavor profiles that might be lacking (sweet or tangy or savory!). I also love working dips onto my boards because most can be made ahead of time so you aren't scrambling to cook right before guests arrive. Your options are endless when it comes to dips, so have fun and play around with flavors to create something truly unique.

When picking out sauces and dips, make sure you know what flavors you will be combining them with. Including some savory cheese and bread? Add a touch of sweetness with a strawberry or fig jam. Featuring salty potato chips? Add a punch of umami with onion or pimento dip.

Prepping & Styling

All sauces and dips should be served in their own small bowls so they don't spread into the other food. Ideally, look for pretty ceramic bowls to keep the presentation top-notch. Make sure each one has its own serving spoon so guests don't accidentally mix flavors when dishing a spoonful onto their plate.

For styling jam, take it out of its original jar (unless the jar is extra pretty) and place it in a small ceramic bowl. Use a spoon to break it apart a bit before putting it out if it's extra thick. That's it—aren't jams easy?!

For dips, I like to use shallow bowls, but the size will depend on how much dip you have to serve—you want the bowl to be full but not overflowing. If the dip is firm enough to spread, my favorite trick is to use the back of a spoon to create a swirl indentation that can be filled with quality olive oil and/ or fresh herbs. To do this, transfer your dip to its shallow serving bowl, lightly press the back of a spoon in the center of the dip, and slowly turn the bowl with your other hand while you gently pull the spoon out- ward to create an even swirl. Drizzle olive oil into the wells and sprinkle with freshly chopped herbs (if there are herbs in the dip) and/or freshly ground black pepper or nice sea salt. If I need to add a little pop of color (usually with tan-colored hummus or something similar), I'll use pink pepper- corns for garnish.

With runnier sauces, I usually serve them in a small shallow glass cup, ceramic gravy boat, or milk pourer since they are easy to find at most stores and come in a range of colors and shapes. Most sauces can be garnished with finely chopped herbs if they need a little extra color.

Dippers:
Bread, Crackers & Chips

I really wanted to call this section *The Vehicle* because the main reason we need carbs (such as bread, crackers, and potato chips) on our spreads is to use them as a vehicle for eating other foods. Although vegetables also work as a vehicle, including some form of carb will add a salty and savory element that brings a new flavor profile and crunchy texture to the food you are serving. If you can't decide which vehicle you like best, give your guests options by laying out a variety of crackers, breads, and chips.

When it comes to bread, look for crusty varieties like baguettes, focaccia, or a country loaf. Day-old bread is better for crostini because some of the moisture has evaporated, ensuring a better crunch.

For crackers, avoid flavors that clash with what you are serving and make sure to consider the texture of the cracker—a buttery cracker will work best with a sharp and hard cheese, while a sturdy option will compliment creamy cheese. Shape and color can add to your overall presentation, so try to pick out a mix of square, triangular, and circular crackers when purchasing. Long cracker sticks also look great on spreads!

For all other chips, search out thick varieties that won't get soggy or snap easily, such as kettle-cooked chips and tortilla chips. You can find a vast selection at almost any grocery store. Growing up, my mom would always serve Katie's Old Fashioned Potato Chips at gatherings because they were local (and delicious, obviously). She's since moved on to Great Lakes Potato Chip Co.—not only is it a special treat for her guests to try a new brand, but it's also such a fun conversation starter since she lives down the road from Lake Michigan.

Prepping

Up to this point, you've been working hard to prepare your gorgeous spread, so I'm going to give you a break with this one—chips and crackers need no prep! As for the bread, if it's not already sliced into bite-size pieces, cut it to accommodate easy handling. If you are worried that the bread might not be sturdy enough, consider toasting it (bonus points if you rub it with a little fresh garlic and olive oil!).

Serving & Styling

You have a couple options when it comes to serving and styling your carbs:

Place each cracker or kind of bread in its own bowl near the food it's meant to be enjoyed with. If you do this, consider picking out the bowls in advance and placing them on the tablescape with the crackers and chips still in their bags and boxes. Before guests arrive, all you have to do is unwrap the items and place them in the bowls. This trick will speed up the final process, ensure you aren't scrambling to find the right bowl at the last minute, and make it less likely that you forget about putting something out since it's already on the table.

The second option is to pile the crackers and bread onto the same platter or board as the items they'll be enjoyed with. This creates a really dramatic spread that feels like it's brimming with options (also known as an abundant spread). To do this, make sure your other food items are already positioned where you want them. Then, fill in any blank space with mounds of bread, crackers, or chips.

Edible Garnish:
Fresh Herbs & Edible Flowers

I'm a firm believer that garnishes and embellishments on your spreads should be edible. I find that nonedible garnishes on boards are a distraction from the food, which should always be the focal point. For this reason, I rely on fresh herbs and edible flowers for my garnishes. I use them to fill in any gaps on a board, to bring in extra color, and to showcase an ingredient that may be used within a recipe (for example, I like to garnish with an herb if a particular dip has that herb in it).

Not only will herbs add bright flavor to the recipes in your spreads, but they will add to the visual presentation as well. If you have the space, consider planting your own small herb garden so you have access to fresh herbs all year round, and you can grow more unusual varieties that might not be available at your local supermarket. I also like to mix in a few edible flowers, such as lavender, daisies, and nasturtiums.

Prepping & Storing

Trim the stems and wash your herbs in cool water as soon as you get home from the store. Trimming will allow for better water absorption, and washing them ahead of time will make your prep easier when you want to use them. Transfer the herbs to a paper towel and roll it up (the paper towel will become damp, which is exactly what we want here). Store in an airtight container or resealable bag in your crisper drawer.

Alternatively, if you have the space on your counter, consider trimming the stems of soft stemmed herbs (such as dill, cilantro, parsley, and mint) and placing them in a glass of water on the counter (like you would a bouquet of flowers). This will free up refrigerator space and will help prevent the herbs from turning brown.

Most herbs should last for up to a week when properly stored.

Styling

Herbs give your board a cohesive feel and keep your theme on point by showcasing some of the ingredients used in your recipes. To garnish with herbs, snip a few sprigs and nestle them in any empty space on your spread. If the leaves are on the larger side, consider tearing them in half before adding.

To keep the board feeling natural, only use herbs and edible flowers when they are in season. For example, use soft-stemmed herbs in the summer like basil, cilantro, and parsley; hardier herbs like sprigs of rosemary and sage in the fall and winter; and chives and thyme in the spring. I also love to garnish with purple basil and orange mint. Just remember to make sure that the garnish makes sense by using herbs and flowers that are in season or in the recipes on the spread.

Garnish

Here are a few of my favorite edible flowers and herbs for garnishing.

PURPLE RUFFLES

BASIL

BORAGE

RED-VEINED SORREL

LEMON THYME

MARIGOLDS

PURPLE SAGE

CHOOSE YOUR OWN ADVENTURE

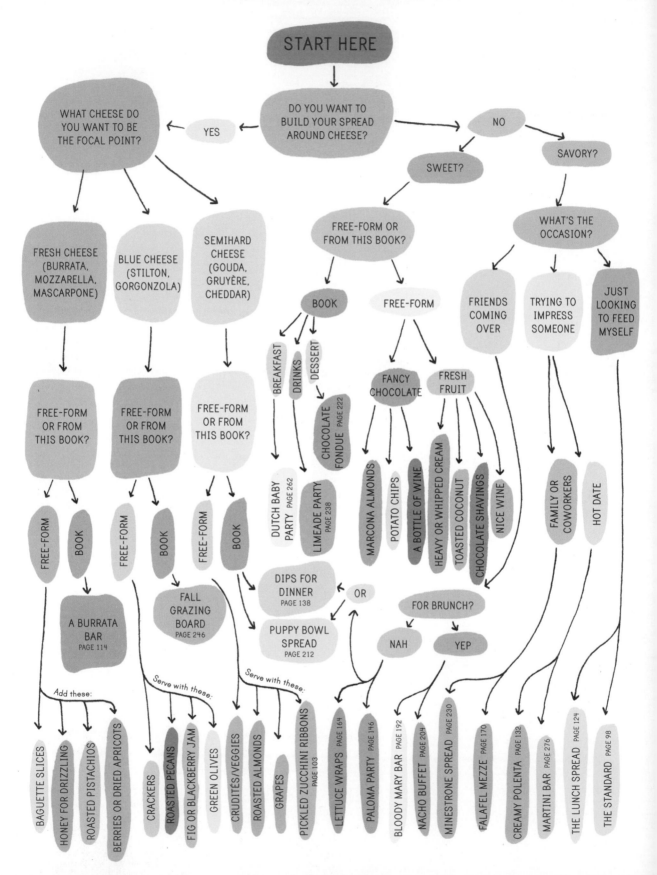

START HERE

DO YOU WANT TO BUILD YOUR SPREAD AROUND CHEESE?

YES

WHAT CHEESE DO YOU WANT TO BE THE FOCAL POINT?

NO

SAVORY?

SWEET?

FREE-FORM OR FROM THIS BOOK?

WHAT'S THE OCCASION?

FRESH CHEESE (BURRATA, MOZZARELLA, MASCARPONE)

BLUE CHEESE (STILTON, GORGONZOLA)

SEMIHARD CHEESE (GOUDA, GRUYÈRE, CHEDDAR)

BOOK

FREE-FORM

FRIENDS COMING OVER

TRYING TO IMPRESS SOMEONE

JUST LOOKING TO FEED MYSELF

FREE-FORM OR FROM THIS BOOK?

FREE-FORM OR FROM THIS BOOK?

FREE-FORM OR FROM THIS BOOK?

BREAKFAST

DRINKS

DESSERT

FANCY CHOCOLATE

FRESH FRUIT

CHOCOLATE FONDUE PAGE 222

FREE-FORM

BOOK

FREE-FORM

BOOK

FREE-FORM

BOOK

DUTCH BABY PARTY PAGE 262

LIMEADE PARTY PAGE 238

MARCONA ALMONDS

POTATO CHIPS

A BOTTLE OF WINE

HEAVY OR WHIPPED CREAM

TOASTED COCONUT

CHOCOLATE SHAVINGS

NICE WINE

A BURRATA BAR PAGE 114

FALL GRAZING BOARD PAGE 246

DIPS FOR DINNER PAGE 138

OR

PUPPY BOWL SPREAD PAGE 212

FOR BRUNCH?

NAH

YEP

FAMILY OR COWORKERS

HOT DATE

Add these:

Serve with these:

Serve with these:

BAGUETTE SLICES

HONEY FOR DRIZZLING

ROASTED PISTACHIOS

BERRIES OR DRIED APRICOTS

CRACKERS

ROASTED PECANS

FIG OR BLACKBERRY JAM

GREEN OLIVES

CRUDITÉS/VEGGIES

ROASTED ALMONDS

GRAPES

PICKLED ZUCCHINI RIBBONS PAGE 103

LETTUCE WRAPS PAGE 164

PALOMA PARTY PAGE 146

BLOODY MARY BAR PAGE 192

NACHO BUFFET PAGE 204

MINESTRONE SPREAD PAGE 230

FALAFEL MEZZE PAGE 170

CREAMY POLENTA PAGE 132

MARTINI BAR PAGE 276

THE LUNCH SPREAD PAGE 124

THE STANDARD PAGE 98

CHECKLIST FOR BUILDING A SPREAD

PICK OUT STAR INGREDIENT OR RECIPE	☐ Star ingredient or recipe is picked out!
SELECT SURFACES AND VESSELS	☐ Got my surface I'm in love with ☐ Trays, platters, and bowls ready to go!
PICK OUT COMPLEMENTARY ITEMS (OPTIONAL IDEAS)	☐ Something salty ☐ Something sweet ☐ Something savory ☐ Something tangy ☐ Vehicle, such as bread or crackers

BASIC ASSEMBLY TIME	☐ Star ingredient
	☐ Items enjoyed with star ingredient added close to it
	☐ Additional filler foods
	☐ Utensils
	   ☐ All cheeses have their own knives
	   ☐ All liquids, spreads, and dips have their own spoons
	   ☐ All meats have their own forks or tongs
	☐ Garnish

Section 3

Adding the Wow Factor

TABLESCAPING

Ready to get into the nitty-gritty details that will bring everything together and take your table from just a countertop for food to an impressive display brimming with character? This next chapter covers all the additional decoration aspects of the table; we'll go over everything from special containers, service ware, and dishes to picking out a color theme and arranging your own floral centerpiece.

I like to call this chapter *Adding the Wow Factor* because I want to make it clear that none of this is necessary to pull off a delicious spread. The things we cover here are for when you really want to go the extra mile and make your grazing table look and feel like a special occasion. Also, feel free to pick and choose parts of this chapter that you'd like to include (maybe a paired-down floral arrangement for that ladies' night you've been meaning to host?) and ditch the parts that don't make sense for your vibe. (Tablecloths—are they necessary? Get my take on page 79.)

WOW-FACTOR SERVEWARE

Pitchers, Drink Dispensers & Decanters

When hosting a crowd, you'll want to make sure you have some drink options handy (even if it's just water!) so folks don't have to rummage through your refrigerator for a can of beer, fill their glass at the sink, or worst of all, come to you each time they need a drink refilled. This is where pitchers, drink dispensers, and decanters come into play.

The pitcher is probably the most versatile of all of these options. It is a must if you are hosting a sit-down dinner, and also usually a good idea if you plan to make batch cocktails like margaritas or sangria. The great thing about pitchers is that you can find them in all sorts of fun shapes and sizes. If serving adults (like in the Time to Celebrate Paloma Party on page 146 or the Boozy Bloody Mary Bar on page 192), I recommend investing in a few nice glass pitchers, which feel more elegant than plastic does. However, if you are serving kids or are hosting an outdoor gathering near a pool (like with the School's Out Summer Limeade Party on page 238), plastic could be the way to go to avoid breakage.

Another outdoor serving option is a drink dispenser with a lid to keep bugs from getting into your batch drink. Drink dispensers are also great for large crowds; they are usually bigger than pitchers, so you won't have to refill them as often. You won't want to place a large dispenser on a table during a sit-down gathering, but they're wonderful during a cocktail party if you can set one up on an out-of-the-way drink table with other beverage options. My favorite way to use a drink dispenser is to fill it with water, fruit, and ice to create infused water, which looks fancy with minimal effort.

Feel free to to use both pitchers and drink dispensers at your gathering. I often have a drink dispenser set up on the appetizer table and then will bring out a pitcher when we sit down for the meal.

Another option is a punch bowl. Punch bowls tend to feel a little bit more classic than drink dispensers. I like to pull them out around the holidays when I want to add a festive touch and know we won't be gathering outside. Punch bowls also make great statement pieces on your table, as they can be filled with decorative ice molds and fruit. Plus, it's not every day that you get to ladle out your drink, so it feels like a novelty for your guests—and frees you up from serving all the drinks! Also, punch glasses are usually small so guests have to refill more often, which gives them a great excuse to congregate around the table and mingle while waiting for their turn.

Finally, if you are serving a nice wine, you'll want to bring out the decanter. Decanting helps separate the wine from any sediment that may have formed in the bottle, and aerates the wine to brighten its flavor and aroma. Not every wine needs decanting, but old reds (15+ years) can benefit from it, as can some newer reds. Older wines should only be decanted for 30 minutes, while younger, full-bodied wines can be decanted an hour or more before serving.

Because there are exceptions to a lot of these rules based on all sorts of wine factors (such as age, grape type, personal prefer-ence, etc.), my rule of thumb is to decant red wine but skip it for white and sparkling wines. (Since I'm not a wine expert in any way, I try to keep it simple.) If you are feel-ing adventurous with your wine, I highly suggest trying it both ways and see which way you prefer!

Other drink-related items you may want to consider for your gathering are ice buckets (place them on the drink station near the other drink supplies) and drink stirrers.

Napkins

Cloth and paper napkins are both well suited for different situations. Cloth nap-kins can feel fancy without you having to do anything more than fold them, while paper ones are a cost-effective option that work great for informal gatherings and cocktail parties.

Cloth Napkins

When I was getting ready to host Thanks-giving for our twenty-five-person family for the first time at my house, my mom told me she was bringing linen napkins as her contribution. To be honest, I was a little annoyed she didn't offer to bring something a little more practical, like the dinner rolls or a pie. When I expressed this annoyance to her, she replied, "Do you have enough cloth napkins for everyone?" When I said no, she assured me that no proper formal event is complete without them. Although I fought it and rolled my eyes, I noticed that the table didn't look complete when I was getting it ready . . . until my mom arrived with the napkins (but don't tell her—I can't have her knowing she was right). They add such a fancy feel to a table setting and yet are often-times overlooked (guilty!) by many hosts.

Another huge plus to cloth napkins is that they are reusable and therefore probably better for the environment than paper ones. If you entertain often, it might be time to invest in some nice cloth napkins that you can easily throw in the wash after a night of heavy eating. You can find them in all sorts of price ranges; look for your new favorite set at local home goods stores for higher-end ones, or go thrifting for a bargain set.

Something else to keep in mind when deciding which to use is what you are serving. Cloth napkins tend to be more durable than paper napkins, so if you are planning to serve something messy like chili or barbecue, then cloth is the way to go.

For most occasions, I recommend picking out a thick cotton material. Cotton napkins lead to easy clean up because they can be thrown into the washing machine with minimal effort (you won't need to hand wash or use a special setting on your machine). I'm a sucker for the look of linen napkins, but they usually have to be ironed to get the wrinkles out. You'll want to factor in extra time for that if going the linen route.

If using cloth napkins, you'll probably want to fold them in some way when setting up your tablescape. You can keep it easy with a simple triangle fold or get all sorts of fancy with your fold technique. On the facing page are three folds that I absolutely love.

If you are planning a formal sit-down event and have enough cloth napkins for the entire table, I highly recommend using them. They can be laid out ahead of time as part of the tablescape and will add a touch of elegance to your party.

Paper Napkins

If you are skipping the dinner-party vibe for something looser like a cocktail party or simple family gathering, paper napkins might be the best option. They are inexpensive and easier to clean up than cloth napkins. They also come in a wide variety of shapes, sizes, and colors to fit any theme.

Another advantage is that they are readily available—you can find fun and unique ones online or just pick up a packet while at the grocery store. When shopping for your event, I recommend estimating needing three or four paper cocktail napkins per guest. These can be set near both the drinks and the spreads for easy access for your guests.

Napkin Folds

THE ANGLED POCKET FOLD

THE ROSEBUD FOLD

THE ENVELOPE

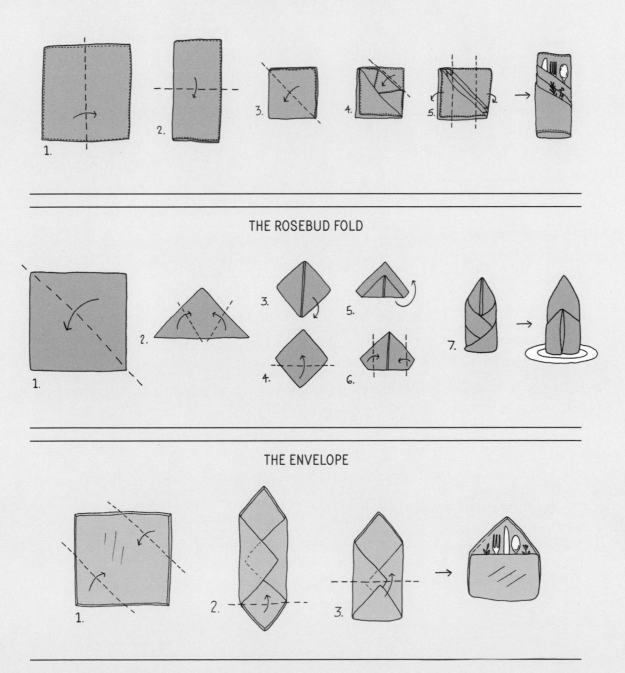

WOW-FACTOR DECORATING

Color Themes

Although there is no right or wrong answer when it comes to choosing colors to use on your table, keeping a uniform color scheme will 1. Give a cohesive feel across your table, and 2. Keep your table from feeling too busy and distracting from the food. Whichever theme you choose, try to stick to no more than one or two main colors and one or two accent colors within that theme to keep from taking attention away from the food. Remember, we want your tablescape to complement the food you are serving, so always think of tableware options as enhancers, not showstoppers.

Here are a few ideas for choosing what colors to incorporate into your tablescape:

Seasonal

One option is to choose a color scheme based on the seasons. For this, select a color you'd like to focus on and then pick one or two complementary colors to use as accents. For spring, you could use muted or pastel colors such as pale yellow, pink, and orange. For summer, use bright hues such as coral, violet, and turquoise. For fall, use warm autumn colors like mustard, deep red, and terra-cotta or burnt orange. For winter, cool blues always look inviting.

See an example of a seasonal color theme on pages 194 to 195.

Once you've chosen a main color for your theme, pick an accent color for your servingware. Silver and black will create a polished tone, while gold and navy will warm up the table.

Neutral

This is my go-to option, which you'll notice when looking at photos throughout this book. Neutral colors are easy to mix and match without having to worry about overwhelming the table. Neutrals also usually allow the colors of the food to pop, which is why you see so many stores selling neutral-hued serving bowls. I love including a mix of neutral pinks, blues, browns, and grays in my tablescapes. This is a great option all year round and can be dressed up or down with accent colors to make it appropriate for every occasion. See an example of a neutral color theme on pages 134 to 135.

Color Spotlight

This option is the trickiest to get right out of all the color schemes because it doesn't take much to make the table look busy and distract from the food. However, when pulled

Color Chart

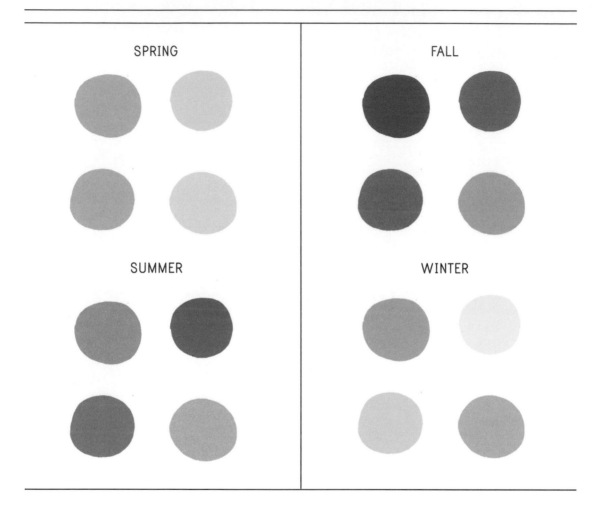

SPRING

FALL

SUMMER

WINTER

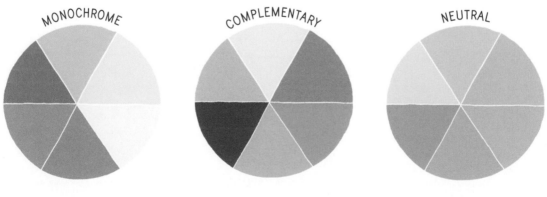

MONOCHROME

COMPLEMENTARY

NEUTRAL

off correctly, you can create a striking scene that really makes your whole table pop. To create a color spotlight tablescape, choose one color as the main focus and then choose one or two complementary or monochromatic colors (see diagram, facing page) and one or two neutral accent colors to include. Choosing monochromatic colors will provide a subtle difference in the colors to create a more cohesive feel. If you'd like the colors to really pop, choose a complementary color (from the color wheel, facing page) as your additional color. See an example of a color spotlight theme on page 76.

Once you've picked out a color theme, you'll want to come back to these colors over and over again when selecting the linens, flowers, candles, serveware, and glasses.

Tablecloths & Runners

Oh, tablecloths—I have such a mixed relationship with you! If I'm being honest, I get so wrapped up in the presentation of the food and the floral arrangement that I often forget to use a tablecloth at all. But just because I don't use them often doesn't mean you shouldn't—it's definitely a personal preference, and probably a good idea to use one if you are planning a formal event.

Using a tablecloth that is on theme with your napkins and tableware can unify your tablescape. By choosing a neutral-colored one, you are allowing the other colors on your table to pop.

Beyond just giving a distinct visual look, they also protect your table from spills and scratches. And they work wonders by covering up blemishes on your tabletop to give the scene a clean and formal look. And finally, they can help reduce noise, as they muffle the sound of glasses or silverware when guests set items down on the table.

A few etiquette rules of thumb: Use a light-colored tablecloth for formal events (think ivory, white, or beige), while informal events are the perfect time to bring out your bright, bold, and/or patterned tablecloths. Use cotton or linen whenever possible, as

Linen Options

Bare Table	Tablecloth	Long Runner
	Tablecloth & Runner	Short Runner

plastic tablecloths give off the feeling of picnicking in the woods (unless, of course, you are trying to go for that camp-y vibe) and should only really be for everyday use and not social events. And, if you have the time, iron your tablecloth before you lay it out; a wrinkle-free tablecloth will help your tablescape look much more put together than a wrinkled one.

If you are new to the world of tablecloths, start with a solid-colored neutral cotton or linen one, which will pair well with most settings. Some heavily patterned table-cloths look fun but can be a big challenge to tablescape with once you start setting items on top of it. And remember (do I sound like a broken record yet?): It's the food we are trying to showcase here, so make sure that your tablecloth enhances the presentation of your dishes and doesn't bury them in a strong pattern or color.

Do you like your table but still want to spruce it up with something more? Let me introduce you to the table runner. Runners come in endless colors and materials and can add extra interest to your table setting without totally taking over. Shorter table runners tend to highlight your centerpiece, while lon-ger ones create a more dramatic look.

If you have a beautiful table that you love to show off (helllooo to my midcentury modern dining table!), then a tablecloth may not be necessary. Also, if the tabletop matches the rest of the tablescape you are using, then even more reason to skip the tablecloth.

Confused about how to choose a tablecloth or runner size?

For casual gatherings, tablecloths should have a 6 to 8 in [15 to 20 cm] drop from the edge of the table to the bottom of the tablecloth. For more formal gatherings, tablecloths should have a 15 in [38 cm] drop. So with this in mind, decide what kind of event you are planning to host, measure your tabletop, and then add either 12 to 16 in [30.5 cm to 40.5 cm] (for a casual get-together) or 30 in [76 cm] for a formal one.

For runners, most come in sizes between 14 and 17 in [35.5 and 43 cm], so choose one that is closest to one-third of the width of your table.

Flowers by Season

Spring	**Summer**
CHERRY BLOSSOMS, PEONIES, DAISIES, LILACS, ROSES, TULIPS, MAGNOLIA, HYDRANGEA, LARKSPUR	DAISIES, LILIES, ZINNIA, SNAPDRAGONS, SUNFLOWERS, POPPIES, GARDENIAS, IRISES
Fall	**Winter**
ROSES, DAHLIAS, MARIGOLDS, CARNATIONS, QUEEN ANNE'S LACE, DAISIES	HOLLY, IVY, MISTLETOE, AMARYLLIS, ROSES, POINSETTIAS, CARNATIONS

Flowers

Coming in second only to the food and spread itself, a floral arrangement will be one of the main focal points on the table. Like creating gorgeous spreads, flower arranging is an art in itself, and all the intricate details could take up an entire book. To keep you from feeling too overwhelmed, I'm just going to share a few simple tips and tricks for creating impactful flower displays with little effort.

But before we jump into arranging, let's talk about the flowers themselves. Although not necessary, choosing in-season flowers will keep your costs lower and feel more in line with your spread (assuming you are using in-season ingredients). Here is a chart of a few common flowers used in arrangements and when they are in season:

Tips for Flower Arrangements

- Know the style and mood you are trying to convey going into it. Tighter bunches of traditional flowers like roses and peonies are going to evoke a classic feel, while lush blooms with irregular stems (like peonies and anemone) will give off more of a whimsical feel.

- Mixing in small, vibrant buds like feverfew and lavender will create a rustic and wild feeling, while creating asymmetrical arrangements with poppies and ranunculus will yield a modern design.

- Think about the colors you want to include; have at least one primary color in mind with one optional complementary color.

- If you can afford it, search out arrangements from a local floral shop or farmers' market. Both places will have unique and in-season selections that will be less common than a drugstore bouquet.

- If you have the budget, you can find reasonably priced options for loose flowers at most grocery stores. I recommend avoiding the pre-mixed bouquets and creating your own with flowers that look the freshest and most vibrant. Keep it simple by picking out two or three different types of flowers in the same color theme, then adding some greenery to fill them out with. Vary the shape of the flowers to create an interesting and well-balanced bouquet. You could even add extra texture with berries or branches if desired.

- As a rule of thumb, your arrangement should be about one and half times the height of the vase.

- Adding greenery is an affordable way to bulk up an arrangement, but creating an all-greenery arrangement can be a gorgeous option if you are on a tight budget or can't find any fresh flowers that strike your fancy.

- One of my other favorite ways to add seasonal touches to floral arrangements is to include fruit branches, such as blueberries on their branches in the summer and figs on their branches in the fall. Mingling food into the arrangements really brings the table together. Other additions include feathers, tall grasses, and herbs from the garden.

- Bud vases are a great option when you'd like to include flowers on your table but are intimidated by creating a bouquet arrangement out of them. Arrange a dozen or so filled bud vases along the center of your table.

- If making an arrangement for a sit-down dinner (versus your grazing table), try to keep the arrangement lower than sitting eye level so guests can still interact with each without having to strain their necks around the display.

- Dry flowers can be used over and over and may be a good option for the fall and winter when local fresh flowers aren't as readily available.

Interested in Making Your Own Floral Arrangement?

It is a fun and creative process that is ideal when you have access to beautiful flowers and greenery. Although it requires a little preparation, the end result can be as visually impactful and rewarding as the homemade food you put on the table.

Pick out your flowers: Head to your local florist, farmers' market, or grocery store. Start by selecting the main color for your arrangement and then choose two or three flowers with varying shades of the same hue. Then pick out a contrasting color to create a pop against the main colors.

Add texture: This is when you'll want to add some greenery and filler such as ferns, eucalyptus, baby's breath, and branches to fill out the arrangement.

Gather your tools: You'll need a vase, floral scissors, clear floral tape, flower food, and a couple of empty buckets. If you are planning to use roses, also gather a thorn stripper. When choosing a vase, make sure you consider the height, volume, and aesthetics of your floral arrangement (which is why I suggest picking out the florals before the vase). Flowers with heavy heads and taller stems will require a vase that can provide support so the flowers don't droop.

Prep your flowers: A few hours before creating the arrangement, carefully unpack your stems and place them in a bucket filled with room-temperature water. If the flowers came with a preservative packet, add this to the water. Trim the stems (just a little for now!) and organize the blooms by type when placing them in the bucket.

Create a grid: Use clear floral tape to create a tic-tac-toe grid across the top of your vase and secure the tape about an inch over the side of the vase (so it is secure but won't be too noticeable once the arrangement is finished). The grid adds support so the flowers stay upright, and will help you space the flowers evenly when building the arrangement.

Prep the flowers: Right before making the arrangement, cut each stem at a 45-degree angle and remove any leaves that will fall below the waterline. The angle gives the flowers more surface area to absorb water so they will hopefully last longer.

Start with greenery: Fill your vase half-way full with water (ideally with plant food in it). Start by adding greenery to each section of your grid.

Add flowers: Start with the larger blooms since they will be the focal point of your arrangement. If you want to make a symmetrical arrangement that looks good from all angles, make sure to turn the vase as you add flowers. Odd numbers of flowers usually looks best, and varying their height adds depth to the arrangement. Then work in smaller accent flowers, grasses, or berries (if using) and any remaining greenery to fill it out.

Candles

Candles not only set an intimate mood by giving off ambient light, but they also add to the overall visual look of your tablescape. Candles come in an array of colors and heights to give extra personality to your dinner for a relatively low cost. Most traditional candles are made from paraffin wax, but soy and beeswax have become popular in recent years as more eco-friendly options. Of course, your budget and what you can find in your area will be the biggest factors in determining what material is best for your gatherings.

Now, which candle type is right for your event? Here are a few of the more common types I use when tablescaping:

Tea Light Candles

Tea light candles are the smallest style of candles. They are great when you want an inexpensive option and don't need to add height to your tablescape. Their compact size makes it easy to add them to an already full table. I like to group them together in clusters to give off more light and ambience. They also work great in decorative glass containers, and they float if you'd like to place them in a bowl of water. Note that most only burn for a few hours, which means you'll want to wait to light them until right before serving the food. Luckily for us, they are usually sold in large packs, so it's easy to replace one if it burns out before your gathering is over.

Taper Candles

These tall and skinny candles are my go-to candles when setting a more formal table. They work beautifully next to a floral centerpiece to create extra height and can be found in endless colors and sizes. I like to spread between three and seven taper candles (depending on how long the table is) across the middle of the table and alternate two different heights. Taper candles can burn for as long as 10 hours, so you don't have to worry about switching them out throughout the gathering. One of the downsides is that they do need a taper candle holder to hold them up, so be sure you purchase some of those when you buy the candles.

Pillar Candles

Pillar candles are big, cylinder-shaped candles that vary in height and diameter. An advantage to these candles is that they don't need special candle holders to stand upright and typically have long-lasting burn times. They are also usually able to light a large area due to their size. I like to buy a few

different sizes of pillar candles and cluster them together on the table, or place them in lanterns or on tiered candle holders.

Music

This will not add to the visuals of your gathering in any way but it will certainly set the mood, so it should not be skipped! If you have a certain kind of music that you and your friends already listen to, then keep to that. If you don't know where to start when it comes to putting music on during a gathering, I always recommend popping on a playlist of either an artist you enjoy (my go-tos are Jenny Lewis and Angel Olsen for low-key vibes or Beyoncé for dance vibes) or pick out a laid-back jazz or soul playlist—two perfect genres for dinner parties. The great thing about letting a music streaming service like Spotify pick the tunes for you is that you don't have to be an expert on any genres to put on a sophisticated playlist for your guests!

Section 4

Anatomy
of a
Spread

A BOARD
FOR EVERY OCCASION

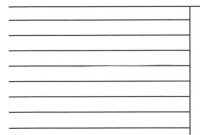

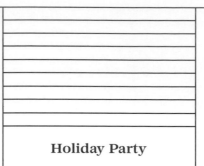

TYPES OF SPREADS

Here are a few notes and tips to keep in mind when setting up
the most common spreads you'll find throughout the book.

Abundance Spread

- Platters or boards
- Pile ingredients high onto each other
- Avoid mixing items! Different types of food can touch, but don't toss them all together and create a salad vibe
- Add tongs or serving toothpicks so guests don't touch the food with their hands
- Serving spoons in each serving bowl
- Place meat off to the side to keep it from mingling with other foods
- Place drink options off to the side
- On grazing table
- Toothpicks, small plates, or napkins for serving

Family Style

- On dining room table
- Place all finished foods and garnishes in small bowls on the table
- Add serving spoons
- Avoid too much space between bowls so it feels full
- Set the table with dinner plates, drink glasses, and silverware
- Create a wow factor with the tablescape (think candles, tablecloth, flowers, etc.)

Statement Piece

- Platters or boards (or a grouping of both)
- One or two star recipes that the board is built around
- Don't overcrowd the star ingredients
- Choose accompaniments based on if they will taste good with the star recipes
- Add utensils for serving
- Place drink options off to the side
- On grazing table
- Toothpicks, small plates, or napkins for serving

Drink Station

- Pitchers for big-batch cocktails
- Glasses for guests
- Drink stirrers for guests
- Place pitchers of drinks, cups, and ice on the far left
- On grazing table
- Garnishes on the right side of the table so guests can finish with them
- Add spoons, forks, or toothpicks for people to use to grab their garnishes

Assembly Spread

- Bowls for ingredient options
- Spoons for ingredient options
- Group similar choices together (for example, garnishes in one area, fillings in another, etc.)
- On work surface with lots of space (such as kitchen counter or dining room table)
- Baking sheet or large plate to put finished items on
- Keep drinks off to the side so they are out of the way

Buffet Style

- Place all food options in nice-looking individual serving bowls
- Put plates and silverware on the far left so people can grab those first
- Organize your food from left to right so that guests can add to their plate in the order you'd like them to
- Serving spoons in each serving bowl
- Place drink options to the far right of the table
- On grazing table

Part 2: Recipes, Boards & Tables

Section 1

Keeping
It Casual

THE STANDARD

By keeping a few nice wedges of cheese, jams, pickled vegetables, and crackers on hand, you'll always be a few minutes away from an easy spread in case unexpected guests decide to stop by on short notice. They will be so impressed that you managed to whip this up in minutes, and you won't even have to break a sweat! Plus, you get to eat the fancy cheese yourself when it's getting close to expiring and you still haven't had guests to share it with. Dinner is served.

Standard does not have to mean boring. This easy, go-to board is anything but with its homemade jam and simple homemade pickles. Make the recipes for this spread if you have time or serve store-bought versions for a quick fix.

Make-Ahead Game Plan

Jam can be made 2 weeks ahead, zucchini pickles 1 week ahead, and nuts up to 3 days ahead. Most fruit can be cut the day before and stored in an airtight container before serving (spritz with some water if it's looking dry). For the day of, crackers can be put out several hours before serving, cheese should be removed from the refrigerator an hour before, cured meat 30 minutes before, and the entire spread can be assembled 15 minutes before serving.

Styling Notes

On the facing page, I give directions for an abundant version or a curated version depending on the look you are going for, the size of the board you'd like to use, and how many people you are entertaining. Make sure you pick out vibrant fruit to bring extra color to the board—I love using fresh deep-purple grapes, figs, or dried apricots.

Drink Pairing

If it's the fall or winter, serve this with a light and dry red wine such as a Gamay or Pinot Noir; they're full of flavor but not so intense that they'll overpower the food. In the spring and summer, serve an even lighter wine like a dry sparkling rosé.

Wyatt's Sidebar

Add slices of a cured meat, such as prosciutto, soppressata, or pepperoni, to bring a punch of umami to your board.

Spread Type

Statement Piece

Choose a special ingredient—maybe a local cheese or homemade jam—for the focus.

Flavor Combination Ideas	Baguette slice + Spicy Cantaloupe Jam (page 100) + Manchego	Cracker + dried apricot + gorgonzola + honey drizzle	Cracker + Gouda + apple slice + honey drizzle

Serves 8

8 oz [230 g] soft or semisoft cheese, such as Brie, chèvre, or Havarti (see page 45)

8 oz [230 g] semihard or hard cheese, such as Gouda, Cheddar, or Manchego (see page 45)

8 oz [230 g] blue cheese, such as Gorgonzola or Stilton (see page 45)

1 cup [340 g] honey or honeycomb

1 cup [275 g] Spicy Cantaloupe Jam (page 100) or your favorite store-bought fruit jam

1 cup [about 330 g] Pickled Zucchini Ribbons (page 103) or your favorite store-bought pickles

2 cups [265 g] Herby Brown Sugar Nuts (page 104) or mixed nuts

1 cup [120 to 140 g] chopped fresh fruit or ½ cup [70 to 90 g] dried fruit (such as grapes, apricots, or apple slices)

8 oz [230 g] assorted brine-cured olives

8 oz [230 g] crackers or 1 baguette, sliced

To create a visually abundant version: On a large serving board, place the cheese pieces in separate areas of the board so they are not touching. Place the honey (or honeycomb), jam, pickles (with some of their liquid), and olives (with some of their liquid) in small serving bowls or rimmed plates and scatter those around the cheese. Fill in all the empty space on the board with the fruits, roasted nuts, and crackers. Place cheese knives near each piece of cheese and spoons in the serving bowls and serve.

To create a board that feels curated: On a large serving board, place the cheese pieces in separate areas of the board so they are not touching. Place the honey (or honeycomb), jam, pickles (with some of their liquid), roasted nuts, and olives (with some of their liquid) in small serving bowls or rimmed plates and scatter those around the cheese. Place the fruit and crackers in their own larger bowls and set those off to the side of the board so as not to take away from the presentation of the cheese. Place cheese knives near each piece of cheese and spoons in the serving bowls and serve.

Spicy Cantaloupe Jam

The cooking time will vary because not all melons have the exact same water content, so make sure you start checking to see if it's set at 25 minutes, and then again every 3 or so minutes after that. I'm also a total wimp when it comes to spice so this recipe is spicy to me, but if you like more heat, feel free to add more red pepper flakes.

Yields 2 cups [555 g]

5 cups [720 g] diced cantaloupe (1 in [2.5 cm] cubes, from 1 large peeled and seeded melon)

1½ cups [300 g] sugar

¼ cup [60 ml] freshly squeezed lemon juice (from 1 large lemon)

½ tsp red pepper flakes

Place the cantaloupe in a medium bowl and toss with the sugar. Let macerate for 30 minutes, tossing the fruit every 10 minutes or so to help encourage the process. Meanwhile, place a small ceramic plate in the freezer.

Pour the melon and all its juices into a large heavy-bottomed pot over high heat. Add the lemon juice and 1 cup [240 ml] of water and bring to a boil, then turn the heat down slightly to medium-high to maintain a low boil and cook for 25 minutes, stirring often.

After 25 minutes, use a potato masher or the back of a fork to break up any large chunks. Check to see if the jam is set by scooping 1 tsp of it onto the ceramic plate from the freezer. Tilt the plate; if the jam slides very slowly and wobbles only slightly, move on to the next step. If it's still too watery, keep boiling. This could take up to an additional 15 minutes depending on how much water your melon had.

Once set, add the red pepper flakes and stir constantly for 1 minute. Remove the pot from the heat and let cool. If you'd like it less chunky, use a potato masher to smash some of the remaining chunks. Transfer the jam to a jar, cover, and chill until ready to serve.

Store, refrigerated in an airtight container, for up to 2 weeks.

Spicy Cantaloupe Jam

Pickled Zucchini Ribbons

A local favorite lunch spot of mine serves similar zucchini pickles on their cheese boards. I always thought the yellow came from curry until I started doing research on pickling and discovered that turmeric has been used as a preservative in Indian food for years. What I love about these zucchini ribbons is that they are very forgiving. Don't have dill on hand? Skip it. Prefer another vinegar? Try apple cider or white wine vinegar. Although I've made these several different ways, the version I include here is my favorite.

Also, in order to end up with a crisp ribbon, it's important that you let them sit in the ice-cold salt mixture and that your brine is close to room temperature when you pour it over the zucchinis (or else they will cook and soften).

Yields 1⅔ cup [555 g]

---

1 lb [455 g] zucchini (about 3 small zucchini), ends trimmed

2 small shallots, ends trimmed and peeled

2 Tbsp salt

1½ cup [360 ml] rice vinegar

1 cup [240 ml] distilled white vinegar (or red wine vinegar or rice vinegar)

1 cup [200 g] sugar

1½ tsp ground mustard

1 tsp yellow mustard seeds

1 tsp ground turmeric

3 sprigs fresh dill

Using a mandolin set to 1.3 mm, slice the zucchini lengthwise to create long ribbon strips. Alternatively, use a large vegetable peeler to slice long lengthwise strips. Slice the shallots.

Transfer the zucchini, shallots, and salt to a shallow 9 by 13 in [23 by 33 cm] casserole dish. Add ice cubes and fill with cold water to cover. Stir until the salt has dissolved, and let sit for 40 minutes.

Meanwhile, in a medium saucepan over high heat, add the vinegars, sugar, ground mustard, mustard seeds, and turmeric and bring to a boil. Lower the heat to low and let simmer for 5 minutes. Remove from the heat and let the mixture cool to room temperature while the zucchini is soaking.

Drain the zucchini and shallots and pat dry. Transfer to a large 6 to 8 cup [1.4 to 2 L] jar or a narrow bowl and add the dill. Pour the cooled brine over the vegetables, making sure to completely cover them. Seal and refrigerate overnight to let the flavors meld.

Serve cold. Store, refrigerated in an airtight container, for up to 1 week.

Herby Brown Sugar Nuts

Feel free to swap in other nuts depending on what you like (macadamia, walnuts, etc.) but stick with rosemary and thyme for the herbs, as there is just something magical that happens when earthy rosemary and thyme mix with sweet brown sugar and salty nuts.

Yields 3¾ cup [500 g]

1½ cups [210 g] raw almonds

1 cup [120 g] pecan halves

½ cup [70 g] raw cashews

3 Tbsp unsalted butter

⅓ cup [65 g] brown sugar

2 Tbsp finely chopped rosemary

1½ tsp chopped thyme leaves

1½ tsp salt

Preheat the oven to 350°F [180°C]. Spread the nuts evenly onto a baking sheet and toast for 10 minutes or until fragrant and beginning to brown. Meanwhile, in a large Dutch oven or saucepan over medium heat, melt the butter. Remove from the heat and whisk in the brown sugar, rosemary, thyme, and salt. Remove the nuts from the oven and transfer to the Dutch oven with the brown sugar mixture. Use a wooden spoon to toss until all the nuts are coated. Transfer back to the baking sheet and spread the nuts in a single layer. Let cool for about 20 minutes before serving.

If not serving the same day, store in an airtight container at room temperature for up to 3 days.

FALL OATMEAL SPREAD

Once the weather starts to chill and apples appear in abundance at the market, cozy up with this board as a comforting fall breakfast for friends and family. Or if you go apple-picking yourself, it even makes for a delicious afternoon reward for everyone who helped you in the orchard.

Styling Notes

For this spread, I rely on layering to really make the presentation pop. I pick three main boards to place on the table (two marble and one wood) and space them out over the table. Next, I use little bowls for most of the mix-ins and scatter them around the boards. I then use one board for garnishes and place the nuts and chocolate directly on the board. I put some of the fruit into bowls and fill in any extra space on the boards with the rest. I love the look of a board spilling onto the table, so sometimes I let a bit of the fruit hang off the board, but you can keep it clean by making sure everything is placed on a board, if you'd prefer.

Drink Pairing

Warm apple cider. Fall is the one time of year that fresh-pressed apple cider pops up at all the grocery stores, so savor the season by warming up a pot to serve with this spread.

Make-Ahead Game Plan

The Spicy Cantaloupe Jam can be made up to 2 weeks ahead of time. Oatmeal can be made up to 2 days ahead of time and reheated (add more water to thin it out). The day before, shave the chocolate, chop the nuts, and toast the coconut; store in airtight containers at room temperature. Reheat the oatmeal and make the Stewed Cardamom Lemon Apples and Caramelized Cinnamon Rum Bananas right before serving.

Spread Type

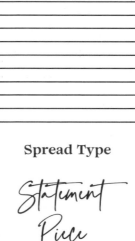

Statement Piece

Flavor Combination Ideas

Oatmeal + Stewed Cardamom Lemon Apples (page 108) + maple syrup + pistachios

Oatmeal + raspberries or grapes + honey + toasted sesame seeds

Oatmeal + Caramelized Cinnamon Rum Bananas (page 111) + almond butter + chopped pecans

Serves 4

6 cups [1.4 L] water or whole milk

½ tsp salt

4 cups [400 g] old-fashioned rolled oats

1 batch Stewed Cardamom Lemon Apples (page 108) and/ or Caramelized Cinnamon Rum Bananas (page 111)

½ cup [150 g] sweet jam (such as Spicy Cantaloupe Jam on page 100, or store-bought)

½ cup [130 g] peanut or almond butter

½ cup [30 g] toasted coconut flakes

¼ cup [85 g] honey

¼ cup [60 ml] maple syrup

1 tsp cinnamon

1 tsp toasted sesame seeds (white or black)

2 cups [240 g] fresh fruit (such as figs, seedless grapes, raspberries, orange slices, etc.)

4 oz [115 g] chocolate shavings

½ cup [60 g] chopped nuts (such as pistachios, almonds, or pecans)

In a large saucepan over medium-high heat, add the water and salt and bring to a boil. Add the oats, lower the heat to medium, and simmer for 3 minutes, stirring often. Remove from the heat, cover, and let sit for 5 minutes. Transfer to a serving bowl and serve warm.

Transfer the Stewed Cardamom Lemon Apples or Cinnamon Rum-Spiced Bananas, jam, nut butter, coconut flakes, honey, maple syrup, cinnamon, and sesame seeds into individual serving bowls. Place three serving boards onto the table and set the bowls of toppings on the three boards. Scatter the fruit, chocolate shavings, and chopped nuts between the bowls on the serving boards to create an abundant spread. Alternatively, place the fruit, chocolate shavings, and chopped nuts in their own serving bowls and scatter the three bowls over a table to serve.

Stewed Cardamom Lemon Apples

Granny Smith apples are a good option for this recipe since they tend to hold their shape better and the tart flavor is the perfect contrast to the brown sugar. You could peel the apples if you'd like, but it's less work if you leave them on, and I personally like the little bit of bite the skin gives.

Yields about 2½ cups [550 g]

---

3 Tbsp unsalted butter

4 tart Granny Smith apples, cut into ¼ in [6 mm] slices

¼ cup [50 g] firmly packed brown sugar

1 tsp cardamom

Pinch of salt

1 tsp lemon zest

¼ tsp vanilla extract

In a 12 in [30 cm] skillet over medium heat, melt the butter. Add the apples and, stirring often, let cook for 5 to 7 minutes or until all the apples have softened. Add the sugar, cardamom, and salt and cook for 30 seconds while stirring to make sure all the apples are coated. Next, add in ½ cup [120 ml] of water, the lemon zest, and vanilla and let simmer, stirring often, for 3 to 4 minutes, or until the liquid is almost completely cooked off. Transfer to a serving bowl and enjoy warm.

These apples are best if enjoyed right away, but leftovers can be stored in an airtight container in the refrigerator for up to 2 days.

Caramelized Cinnamon Rum Bananas

This recipe comes together quickly, so make sure you have a timer nearby and all your ingredients ready!

Yields about 2 cups [400 g]

---

2 Tbsp unsalted butter

3 Tbsp brown sugar

½ tsp cinnamon

3 ripe but firm bananas, halved, then cut in half lengthwise

¼ cup [60 ml] dark rum

In a 12 in [30 cm] nonstick skillet over medium heat, melt the butter. Sprinkle the sugar and cinnamon over the melted butter. Lay the banana slices, cut-side up, over the sugar mixture and cook for 25 seconds before splashing in the rum. Cook for 10 seconds, flip the bananas, and cook for another minute. Use tongs to transfer the bananas onto a serving platter and drizzle any lingering sauce from the skillet over the bananas. Serve warm.

The bananas lose their texture over time, so make this dish right before serving.

A BURRATA BAR

I purposefully added several different simple seasonal salad options to this spread so you can make it all year round. This allows you to just put together the salad that is in season or go for them all. To make this bar work with just one salad, triple the salad recipe and consider gearing some of your other topping options toward that season (such as strawberry jam and basil for summer, apple butter and rosemary for fall, etc.).

Spread Type

Assembly Spread

Drink Pairing

Pick out a few Italian wines to keep with the theme—I'd recommend having one sparkling, one white, and one red on hand if you can.

Wyatt's Sidebar

Serve slices of prosciutto as a topping option in case guests would like to include a little protein in their burrata creations.

Styling Notes

Choose a variety of colors when picking out produce for this section (for example, try to seek out heirloom tomatoes in different colors or both red and yellow beets). You can also either place the burrata out on its own by the salads, or divide the burrata between three bowls and add some of the salad to the bowls to create a sort of pre-made spread so your guests just need to add garnishes.

Make-Ahead Game Plan

Salads can be made the morning of and stored in the refrigerator in an airtight container until ready to serve. Wait until serving to add the burrata.

Flavor Combination Ideas

Baguette slice + burrata + Spicy Cantaloupe Jam (page 100) + olives

Cracker + Citrus & Red Onion Salad (page 121) + mint

Baguette slice + Spicy Cherry Tomato & Cucumber Salad with Basil (page 122).

Serves 12

24 oz [680 g] burrata (three 8 oz
  [230 g] balls or six 4 oz [115 g] balls)

1 batch Shaved Beet & Carrot Salad
  with Sumac & Dill (page 118)

1 batch Citrus & Red Onion Salad
  (page 121)

1 batch Spicy Cherry Tomato &
  Cucumber Salad with Basil
  (page 122)

1 cup Spicy Cantaloupe Jam (page 100)
  or your favorite jam

3 cups [480 g] marinated olives

1 cup [20 to 25 g] mixed seasonal
  herbs (such as basil, mint, rosemary,
  and dill)

12 oz [340 g] crackers

1 baguette, sliced

Salt and pepper, for serving

Start by placing the burrata into its own bowl and setting it on the left side of the grazing table. Place all the salads into individual serving bowls and add those to the right of the cheese. Place all the remaining topping and garnish options into their own individual bowls and set them out to the right of the salads. Make salt and pepper available on the table and serve.

Shaved Beet & Carrot Salad with Sumac & Dill

This salad is perfect for fall and winter when root vegetables are in abundance. Since both beets and carrots can be rather tough raw, slice the beets and carrots as thinly as possible (using either a mandolin or your hands) to create a delicious crunch.

Serves 4

---

5 medium beets, peeled and thinly sliced

4 carrots, peeled and thinly sliced

1 Tbsp white wine vinegar

1 Tbsp finely chopped dill, plus more for serving

2 tsp Dijon mustard

1 tsp sumac

½ tsp salt, plus more for seasoning

¼ cup [60 ml] olive oil

Freshly ground black pepper

8 oz [230 g] burrata (optional)

Crackers, for serving (optional)

In a large bowl, toss together the sliced beets and carrots and set aside.

In a small mixing bowl, whisk together the vinegar, dill, mustard, sumac, and salt. Continue to whisk while pouring the olive oil into the bowl until emulsified. Season with salt and pepper.

Drizzle the dressing over the beet and carrot mixture and toss to coat. Taste and season with more salt and pepper before transferring to a shallow serving bowl.

If serving this salad on its own, tear and arrange the burrata over the salad and serve with crackers.

Shaved Beet
& Carrot Salad
with Sumac &
Dill

Citrus & Red Onion Salad

Make this salad in the winter when you are able to snag a variety of oranges so that the end result has a beautiful variety of hues of red and orange.

Serves 4

¼ cup [35 g] thinly sliced red onions

¼ cup [60 ml] red wine vinegar

3 medium or 4 small oranges (ideally a mix of blood orange, navel, and Cara Cara), peeled and cut into segments or rounds

2 Tbsp olive oil

¼ tsp salt, plus more for seasoning

Dash of freshly ground black pepper, plus more for seasoning

¼ cup [35 g] chopped green olives

2 Tbsp chopped pistachios

½ Tbsp packed tarragon

8 oz [230 g] burrata (optional)

Crackers, for serving (optional)

In a small bowl, cover the red onions with the vinegar. Set aside to let mellow for at least 10 minutes. Strain, reserving 1 Tbsp of the vinegar.

Arrange the oranges in a shallow serving bowl and set aside.

In a small mixing bowl, whisk together the reserved vinegar, the olive oil, salt, and pepper. Add the green olives, pistachios, and tarragon and toss together to coat everything in the olive oil mixture.

Spread the onions over the oranges and spoon the pistachio mixture over the onions and oranges. Drizzle any remaining liquid from the pistachio mixture bowl into the serving bowl. Taste and add more salt and pepper, if needed.

If serving this salad on its own, tear and arrange the burrata over the salad and serve with crackers.

Spicy Cherry Tomato & Cucumber Salad with Basil

I like to use cherry tomatoes here, as they won't get the salad too watery and are easy to find in most seasons (although this one will be extra delicious on a hot summer day when basil and cucumbers are in abundance in the garden).

Serves 4

1½ cups [240 g] cherry tomatoes (ideally a mix of colors), halved

½ English cucumber, cut into ½ in [12 mm] dice

1 jalapeño, seeded and minced

2 Tbsp olive oil

1 Tbsp freshly squeezed lemon juice

¼ tsp salt, plus more for seasoning

Dash of freshly ground black pepper, plus more for seasoning

2 Tbsp torn basil

8 oz [230 g] burrata (optional)

Crackers, for serving (optional)

In a medium mixing bowl, toss together the tomatoes, cucumber, and jalapeño.

In a small mixing bowl, whisk together the olive oil, lemon juice, salt, and pepper. Drizzle the mixture over the vegetables and toss to make sure all the veggies are coated.

Add the basil and season with more salt and pepper, if needed.

If serving this salad on its own, tear and arrange the burrata over the salad and serve with crackers.

THE LUNCH SPREAD

Make the farro salad (I love to make a batch on Sundays and enjoy it in the early week) and cut the veggies ahead of time to cut down on prep time for this spread. Use ricotta or Greek yogurt to make a quick "dip" (you're really just lightly flavoring them) for the veggies and whip up a batch of Cacio e Pepe 7-Minute Eggs (page 130) for protein. This serves two, but feel free to save some of it as leftovers for the next day if it's only for one.

Spread Type

Abundance Spread

Wyatt's Sidebar

To add a dose of extra protein to this spread, crumble a few pieces of cooked bacon into the farro salad—it will go great with the pecans and blue cheese!

Flavor Combination Ideas

Eat the Roasted Leek, Apple & Blue Cheese Farro Salad (page 128), Cacio e Pepe 7-Minute Eggs (page 130), and roasted nuts by themselves, but enjoy the Homemade Ricotta (page 220) on a slice of fresh bread with a few pieces of veggies and a sprinkle of fresh herbs.

Styling Notes

Since this is serving only two people, you won't need too big of a board here. Use a small serving platter or large dinner dish (may I suggest something neutral colored?). Place the ricotta or yogurt in the middle of the dish and then pile all the other components around it. You could also serve the salad on the plate if you have room, or put it in its own bowl on the side.

Drink Pairing

Enjoy with sparkling water. If you're feeling extra fancy, add a few tablespoons (depending on how sweet you like it) of blueberry lemon simple syrup (see page 151) or raspberry ginger simple syrup (see page 152) and some fresh fruit (like lemon slices or fresh berries).

Make-Ahead Game Plan

Eggs can be cooked 3 days ahead of time and stored in the refrigerator. Both the Homemade Ricotta (page 220) and the Roasted Leek, Apple & Blue Cheese Farro Salad (page 128) can be made up to 2 days ahead of time (but let the salad come to room temperature before serving). Vegetables can be chopped a day ahead and stored in an airtight container in the refrigerator (spritz with water before serving if they are starting to look dry). The spread can be assembled up to 30 minutes before serving.

Serves 2

½ cup [120 g] Homemade Ricotta (page 220) or Greek yogurt

1 Tbsp olive oil

1 tsp chopped fresh herbs (such as thyme leaves and basil)

Salt and freshly ground black pepper

3 cups [545 g] Roasted Leek, Apple & Blue Cheese Farro Salad (page 128)

1 batch Cacio e Pepe 7-Minute Eggs (page 130)

2 cups [240 to 320 g] fresh raw vegetables, chopped into bite-size pieces (such as carrots, cucumbers, radishes, bell pepper slices, endive, cherry tomatoes, celery, etc.)

2 slices fresh bread (such as sourdough or focaccia, toasted if you'd like) or 2 oz [55 g] crackers

¼ cup [35 g] roasted nuts (such as pistachios, almonds, pecans, etc.)

Place the Homemade Ricotta in a small serving bowl and top it with the olive oil and fresh herbs (see page 59 for my swirl technique). Season with salt and pepper. Place the bowl in the center of your serving plate.

Place the Roasted Leek, Apple & Blue Cheese Farro Salad in a nice serving bowl and set it next to the serving platter. Fill in the remaining space on the platter with the egg halves, vegetables, bread, and nuts. Serve right away.

Leek, Apple &
Blue Cheese
Farro Salad

Roasted Leek, Apple & Blue Cheese Farro Salad

This salad is even more delicious the day after you prepare it because the farro absorbs more of the flavors from the dressing.

Yields about 5½ cups [1000 g]

For the dressing

¼ cup [60 ml] olive oil

1 Tbsp white wine vinegar

1 tsp chili garlic sauce (such as Huy Fong Foods) or your favorite hot sauce

1 tsp honey

½ tsp salt

⅛ tsp freshly ground black pepper

For the salad

1 cup [180 g] farro, rinsed

1½ tsp salt, plus more for seasoning

One 15 oz [430 g] can chickpeas, drained and rinsed

2 Tbsp olive oil

1 small leek, trimmed, washed, halved, and sliced into ½ in [12 mm] half-moons

⅓ cup [40 g] pecan halves

1 tart apple, cored and diced

¼ cup [35 g] yellow raisins

¼ cup [30 g] crumbled blue cheese

Freshly ground black pepper

Set up two racks in the oven and preheat the oven to 400°F [200°C]. Line two baking sheets with parchment paper.

To make the dressing, whisk together the olive oil, vinegar, chili garlic sauce, honey, salt, and pepper in a small mixing bowl. Set aside.

To make the salad, in a medium saucepan over high heat, add the farro, ½ tsp of the salt, and 4 cups [960 ml] of water and bring to a boil. Lower the heat medium-low and let simmer for 20 to 25 minutes or until the farro is tender. Drain any excess water and set aside.

Meanwhile, add the chickpeas to one of the prepared baking sheets and toss with 1 Tbsp of the olive oil and ½ tsp of the salt. Spread into an even layer and bake for 10 minutes on the bottom rack of the oven.

Place the leeks on the other baking sheet and toss with the remaining 1 Tbsp of olive oil and the remaining ½ tsp of salt and then spread the leeks into an even layer.

Pour the chickpeas (which have baked for 10 minutes) on top of the leeks and place the sheet on the top rack of the oven. Bake for an additional 10 minutes or until both the leeks and chickpeas are brown. Use a spatula to push the chickpea mixture to one side of the baking sheet and add the pecans. Let bake for another 3 minutes or until fragrant. Remove both baking sheets from the oven and set aside.

Once the pecans are cool enough to chop, roughly chop and place them in a large mixing bowl.

In the same large mixing bowl, add the cooked farro, chickpeas, leeks, apple, raisins, and blue cheese and mix to combine. Drizzle in the dressing and mix again. Taste and add more salt or pepper, as needed.

This salad can be made up to 2 days ahead and stored in an airtight container in the refrigerator. Let the salad come back to room temperature when serving.

Cacio e Pepe 7-Minute Eggs

Love cheesy eggs? Then this recipe is for you! Mayo stands in for pasta water to give these eggs the extra-creamy richness that you usually find in traditional Cacio e Pepe. Using two different grating methods for the cheese allows some of it to melt while some stays firm, providing a variety of textures. I give my preferred ratio of cheese and mayo to egg in this recipe, but play around and add more or less depending on how rich you'd like these to be.

Serves 2

---

2 eggs

2 tsp mayonnaise

2 oz [55 g] shaved Parmesan cheese

2 tsp grated Parmesan cheese

Freshly ground black pepper

Bring a saucepan filled with water to a rapid boil over high heat. Using a slotted spoon, lower the eggs into the water and lower the heat to medium or medium-low so that the water maintains a simmer. Let simmer for 7 minutes.

Meanwhile, make an ice bath by placing 2 cups [280 g] of ice in a medium bowl and covering with water. When the eggs are done, transfer them to the ice bath and let cool for at least 2 minutes.

Crack and peel the eggs. Slice them in half and smear ½ tsp of the mayonnaise on the cut side of each half. Top each with ½ oz shredded Parmesan, ½ tsp grated Parmesan, and a half-turn of pepper. Serve right away.

Eggs can be cooked and stored, unpeeled, in the refrigerator for up to 3 days before serving. Peel and assemble them right before serving.

CREAMY POLENTA SPREAD

Most of the spreads in this book are for your grazing table, but a few (like this one!) would also work great as a sit-down dinner (or brunch!). If you plan to make both polenta recipes for this spread, you can take a little shortcut by cooking a double batch of polenta and then dividing it in half after cooking for 30 minutes but before adding in the additional flavors.

Styling Notes

You've got two options with this one: You could serve this as a main meal for a small group, or you could make a little buffet if you want to treat it as a snack or starter. If going with the former, serve it family style with the table set (head back to page 30 for tablescape inspiration) and all the components in serving bowls on the dining room table. If serving as a grazing option, make a grazing table off to the side of your dining room or kitchen and create an assembly line (from left to right) by setting out serving bowls and utensils followed by the polenta and then little shallow bowls filled with all the topping options.

Make-Ahead Game Plan

Polenta can be made 3 hours ahead and stored, covered, in the refrigerator. Reheat over low heat, adding more water to loosen the polenta. The bell peppers, onions, and kale can be sautéed 1 hour ahead, and all the toppings (minus the eggs) can be put out 30 minutes ahead. Wait to reheat the polenta and cook the eggs until right before serving.

Spread Type

Buffet Style or Family Style

Drink Pairing

Serve with a dry red wine like Cabernet Sauvignon or Merlot. Or if you want to serve this for brunch, whip up a batch of mimosas by mixing together two parts orange juice and one part sparkling wine.

Wyatt's Sidebar

Add cooked sweet Italian sausage to create an even heartier meal. This would work great with either of the polentas, sautéed peppers and onions, kale, and marinara sauce.

Flavor Combination Ideas

Creamy Mascarpone Polenta (page 136) + bell peppers and onions + kale + chickpeas + marinara sauce + parsley

Pumpkin Ricotta Polenta (page 137) + bell peppers and onions + kale + fried eggs + pesto

Creamy Mascarpone Polenta (page 136) + bell peppers and onions + kale + black beans + buffalo sauce + cilantro

Serves 4 as a main, 8 to 10 as a snack or appetizer

1 batch Creamy Mascarpone Polenta (page 136) or Pumpkin Ricotta Polenta (page 137)

2 Tbsp olive oil

1 red or yellow bell pepper, sliced into thin strips

1 onion, sliced into thin rings

1 tsp salt, plus more for seasoning

1 bunch kale, stems removed, roughly torn into bite-size pieces

2 Tbsp unsalted butter

4 eggs

Freshly ground black pepper

½ cup [120 g] pesto

½ cup [120 g] marinara sauce

¼ cup [60 g] buffalo sauce

¼ cup [10 g] chopped cilantro

¼ cup [10 g] chopped parsley

One 15 oz [430 g] can black beans, drained and warmed

One 15 oz [430 g] can chickpeas, drained and warmed

Prepare the polenta and keep warm over low heat. In a medium nonstick skillet over medium heat, warm 1 Tbsp of the olive oil. Add the bell peppers, onion, and ½ tsp of the salt and saute for 5 to 7 minutes or just until the vegetables begin to soften. Remove from skillet and set aside.

Turn the heat down to medium-low, warm the remaining 1 Tbsp of olive oil in the skillet, and add the kale and the remaining ½ tsp of salt. Let cook for about 5 minutes, tossing often, until softened but not soggy. Remove from the skillet and set aside.

Add the butter to the same skillet. Once melted, crack the eggs into different sections of the skillet (being careful not to let them overlap, if possible). Cover and let cook for 3 minutes. Remove the lid, tilt the skillet slightly so all the excess butter falls to one side, and use a spoon to splash the pooled butter over any unset egg whites (this will help them cook). Remove from the heat and season with salt and pepper.

To assemble, put the eggs on a plate and the bell peppers, onion, kale, polenta, pesto, marinara, buffalo sauce, cilantro, parsley, black beans, and chickpeas in their own serving bowls. Arrange either family style or buffet style (see styling notes, facing page).

Creamy
Mascarpone

Pumpkin
Ricotta

Creamy Mascarpone Polenta

The mascarpone helps create a rich and creamy polenta that is perfect for any time of year.

Serves 4

---

1 tsp salt, plus more for seasoning

1 cup [140 g] polenta

½ cup [120 g] mascarpone

2 Tbsp unsalted butter

2 Tbsp grated Parmesan cheese

Freshly ground black pepper

In a large saucepan over high heat, bring 4 cups [960 ml] of water and the salt to a boil. Gradually whisk in the polenta and lower the heat to medium–low to simmer for 5 minutes, stirring often, until the polenta starts to thicken. Cover and let cook for 30 minutes, stirring every 5 minutes or so, or until the polenta is thick and creamy and no longer chewy or hard when you sample it. Remove from the heat and stir in the mascarpone, butter, and Parmesan. Season with pepper and more salt, if needed.

Polenta can be made 3 hours ahead and stored, covered, in the refrigerator. Reheat over low heat, adding more water to loosen the consistency.

Pumpkin Ricotta Polenta

Love sneaking vegetables into your dishes? Me too! Sneaking the puréed pumpkin into this recipe not only makes it taste like fall but also gives a deliciously creamy texture to the polenta.

Serves 4

1 tsp salt, plus more for seasoning

1 cup [140 g] polenta

½ cup [120 g] canned pumpkin

½ cup [120 g] Homemade Ricotta (page 220) or store-bought

2 Tbsp unsalted butter

⅛ tsp nutmeg

Freshly ground black pepper

In a large saucepan over high heat, bring 4 cups [960 ml] of water and the salt to a boil. Gradually whisk in the polenta and lower the heat to medium-low to simmer for 5 minutes, stirring often, until the polenta starts to thicken. Cover and let cook for 30 minutes, stirring every 5 minutes or so, or until the polenta is thick and creamy and no longer chewy or hard when you sample it. Remove from the heat and stir in the pumpkin, ricotta, butter, and nutmeg. Season with pepper and more salt, if needed.

Polenta can be made 3 hours ahead and stored, covered, in the refrigerator. Reheat over low heat, adding more water to loosen the consistency.

DIPS FOR DINNER

My favorite dinner on a lazy night is a spread of made-ahead dips and fresh vegetables because it's always a little bit different depending on what veggies I have in the refrigerator. If you aren't planning to serve a larger group of people, feel free to cut this down to one dip to make it a hearty meal for two, or make all the dips and save some for leftovers.

Styling Notes

Make sure to reference the tips in part 1 about how to make your vegetables look as beautiful as possible (see page 53) and transfer the dips into nice serving bowls to give the meal an extra-special touch.

Drink Pairing

Serve with light and refreshing gin and tonics for an easy alcoholic option, or just soda water with a little blueberry lemon simple syrup (see page 151) for a fun nonalcoholic option.

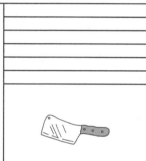

Wyatt's Sidebar

This spread is a great opportunity to include a few tins of high-quality canned fish, such as anchovies or tuna.

Make-Ahead Game Plan

Smoky Sun-Dried Tomato & Walnut Dip (page 141) can be made 2 days ahead and stored in an airtight container in the refrigerator. The day before, make the Blackberry-Dijon Whipped Ricotta (page 142), chop the raw vegetables, and store both in individual airtight containers in the refrigerator (if the vegetables look dry when you're ready to serve, spritz them with some water). The spread can be assembled, including transferring dips to serving bowls, 30 minutes ahead of serving.

Spread Type

Abundance Spread or Statement Piece

Serves 6 to 8 as a main

1 batch Smoky Sun-Dried Tomato &
Walnut Dip (page 141)

1 batch Blackberry-Dijon Whipped
Ricotta (page 142)

1 batch White Cheddar & Green Chili
Pinto Dip (page 145)

4 oz [115 g] olives or pickled
vegetables

½ cup [70 g] toasted nuts

12 cups [1.9 kg] raw vegetables, cut
into bite-size pieces (such as cherry
tomatoes, celery sticks, carrots,
bell pepper strips, broccoli florets,
cauliflower florets, snap peas,
endive, etc.)

8 oz [230 g] potato chips or crackers

6 slices toasted bread or pita

Sea salt and freshly ground black
pepper, for serving

Arrange serving bowls of the dips on a large serving platter or board, leaving space between each bowl. Place the olives and/or pickled vegetables and toasted nuts in their own small bowls and add them to the platter. Arrange the remaining items around the platter, filling in any empty space to create an abundant spread. Add small dishes of salt and pepper to the side.

Sun-Dried Tomato
& Walnut Dip

Smoky Sun-Dried Tomato & Walnut Dip

Inspired by one of my favorite romesco recipes, this dip is full of smoky flavor and texture. When pulsing all the ingredients together, make sure to keep this dip a little chunky so you can still enjoy some of the crunch from the walnuts.

Yields about 1½ cups [355 g]

---

1 cup [120 g] walnut halves

1 roasted red pepper (about 6 oz [170 g]) from a water-packed jar

½ cup [100 g] sun-dried tomatoes (from an oil-packed jar)

1 or 2 canned chipotle peppers in adobo sauce (depending on your affinity for heat)

1 garlic clove, finely minced

2 Tbsp freshly squeezed lemon juice

2 Tbsp olive oil

½ Tbsp adobo sauce (from the can of chipotle peppers), plus more as needed

½ tsp salt

½ tsp smoked paprika

Freshly ground black pepper

Preheat the oven to 350°F [180°C] and lay out the walnuts in a single layer on a baking sheet. Toast for 7 to 8 minutes, tossing halfway through, or until the walnuts have darkened and are omitting a nutty aroma. Let cool and roughly chop.

Place the chopped walnuts, red pepper, sun-dried tomatoes, chipotle pepper, garlic, lemon juice, 1 Tbsp of the olive oil, the adobo sauce, salt, and paprika in a food processor and pulse 15 times or just until a chunky consistency has formed. Taste and add more adobo sauce if it's not hot enough for you. Transfer to a serving bowl and drizzle with the remaining 1 Tbsp of olive oil and the black pepper (see page 59 for my swirl technique).

The dip can be stored in an airtight container in the refrigerator for up to 2 days. Wait to drizzle with the olive oil and black pepper until right before serving.

Blackberry–Dijon Whipped Ricotta

Creamy and sharp all at once, this will be a purple-tinged offering when blended.

Yields about 2 cups [530 g]

½ cup [150 g] seedless blackberry jam

1 Tbsp Dijon mustard

1½ tsp red wine vinegar

1 tsp freshly squeezed lemon juice

½ tsp salt

⅛ tsp freshly ground black pepper

2 cups [440 g] Homemade Ricotta (page 220) or store-bought

1 Tbsp olive oil

⅛ tsp freshly ground pink peppercorns, for serving (or more black pepper)

In a small bowl, whisk together the jam, mustard, vinegar, lemon juice, salt, and black pepper. Set aside.

Using a stand mixer fitted with the whisk attachment, whip the ricotta on high speed for 2 minutes. With the mixer running on medium-low speed, slowly pour in the jam mixture. Continue to whisk for another minute or until the blackberry jam is completely incorporated into the ricotta.

Transfer the ricotta mixture to a shallow serving bowl, press it down into an even layer, and top it with the olive oil and pink peppercorns (see page 59 for my swirl technique).

This dip can be made a day ahead of time and stored in an airtight container in the refrigerator. Wait to drizzle with the olive oil and pink peppercorn until right before serving.

White Cheddar & Green Chili Pinto Dip

This flavorful bean dip is delicious eaten with crisp, raw veggies, tortilla chips, and even stuffed into tacos.

Yields 2 cups [480 g]

1 Tbsp olive oil

1 small red onion, diced

2 garlic cloves, minced

One 15 oz [430 g] can pinto beans, drained and rinsed

1 tsp chili powder

½ tsp smoked paprika

One 7 oz [200 g] can diced green chilis

½ tsp salt

¾ cup [60 g] shredded white Cheddar cheese

Tortilla chips, for serving

In a small saucepan over medium heat, warm the olive oil. Add the onion and sauté for 5 minutes or until it starts to soften. Add the garlic and sauté for 30 seconds. Add the beans, chili powder, and smoked paprika and sauté for another 30 seconds.

Transfer the bean mixture to a food processor fitted with the blade attachment. Add the diced green chilis (including their juices) and salt. Process until smooth, about 20 seconds.

Transfer the dip back into the small saucepan and turn the heat to medium. Stir in ½ cup [40 g] of the Cheddar and stir until completely melted, about 30 seconds.

Remove from the heat and transfer the dip to a serving bowl. Top with the remaining ¼ cup [20 g] of Cheddar and serve with tortilla chips. Store leftover dip in an airtight container in the refrigerator for up to 3 days.

TIME TO CELEBRATE PALOMA PARTY

Whatever you might be celebrating (a birthday, Cinco de Mayo, payday, whatever!), big-batch palomas are almost always a good idea. Interested in earning extra points? Pull out the blender and whip up paloma slushies alongside the big-batch versions. Also, if your guests like their drinks on the sweeter side, consider topping the rim with agave along with lime juice and salt for an added layer of sweet.

Make-Ahead Game Plan

Simple syrups can be made up to 1 week ahead of time. The citrus juices can be squeezed the day before and stored in an airtight container in the refrigerator. The citrus can be sliced the morning of (spritz it with water right before serving if it looks dry), and the big-batch recipes can be mixed (minus the sparkling water) several hours before. Assemble the board 15 minutes before serving and add the sparkling water and ice right before guests arrive. Wait to make the Raspberry Ginger Paloma Slushies (page 152) until a guest requests one.

Wyatt's Sidebar

Add a few strips of crumbled bacon to the guacamole for an extra salty crunch.

Styling Notes

Use clear pitchers (made of glass, if you have them) to let the beautiful color of the palomas shine through on the serving table.

Spread Type

Drink Station

Snack Pairing

Serve with chips and guacamole (such as the Loaded Guacamole on page 209).

Serves 12

1 batch **Big-Batch Palomas** (page 150)

1 batch **Big-Batch Blueberry Lemon Palomas** (page 151) **or 6 Raspberry Ginger Paloma Slushies** (page 152)

12 **grapefruit slices or wedges (from 3 grapefruits)**

12 **lemon slices or wedges (from 3 lemons)**

12 **lime slices or wedges (from 3 limes)**

1 **cup [140 g] blueberries**

¼ **cup [55 g] salt**

Ice, for serving

Transfer the Big-Batch Palomas and the Big-Batch Blueberry Lemon Palomas to their own pitchers and place them toward the back of a serving tray. Place the grapefruits, lemons, limes, and blueberries in their own individual bowls and set them in front of the pitchers on the serving tray. Alternatively, you can put the citrus slices directly on your serving dish if there is room.

Spread out the salt on a small dish and rub the rims of 12 glasses with one of the lime, lemon, or grapefruit slices. Dip each glass into the salt so that the rim gets coated and place the glasses near the tray. Reserve the remaining salt for another use or set it off to the side in case you make a few more paloma batches later.

Place small forks or serving utensils with the fruit so that guests can easily add the garnish to their drinks.

If guests will be enjoying the drinks right away, feel free to also put out a bucket of extra ice. If not, just let them know they can find more in the freezer. If serving the Raspberry Ginger Paloma Slushies, let your guests know they are an option and make on request.

Big-Batch Palomas

Why mess with additional flavoring when the classic is just so darn delicious? This recipe is perfect for when you want to keep it traditional.

Serves 6 to 8

For the simple syrup

½ cup [100 g] sugar

For the palomas

4 cups [960 ml] sparkling water

2 cups [480 ml] freshly squeezed grapefruit juice (from 4 large grapefruits)

12 fl oz [360 ml] tequila

½ cup [120 ml] freshly squeezed lime juice (from 4 limes)

Salt, for rimming the glasses

Grapefruit wedges, for garnish

First, make the simple syrup. In a small saucepan over medium-high heat, bring the sugar and ½ cup [120 ml] of water to a boil. Lower the heat to medium and let simmer for 2 minutes, stirring often, until all the sugar has dissolved. Remove from the heat and let cool. The simple syrup can be made up to 1 week ahead of time and stored in an airtight container in the refrigerator.

To make the palomas, in a pitcher, combine the sparkling water, grapefruit juice, tequila, lime juice, and simple syrup.

Pour a mound of salt onto a small dish that is slightly larger than your glasses and rub one of the grapefruit wedges around the rim of your glasses. Dip the rim of each glass in the salt mound.

Fill the salt-rimmed glasses with ice and pour in the paloma mixture. Garnish with grapefruit wedges.

Big-Batch Blueberry Lemon Palomas

These are slightly sweeter than the regular big-batch palomas (we use more simple syrup to really bring out the blueberry flavor), but I like that my guests can have options in case they prefer sweeter or tarter cocktails. You'll start by using only two-thirds of the simple syrup and then adjusting to taste by adding more later if you think it should be sweeter once everything is combined.

Serves 6 to 8

For the simple syrup

1 cup [200 g] sugar

1 cup [140 g] fresh blueberries

⅓ cup [80 ml] freshly squeezed lemon juice

Zest of 1 lemon

For the palomas

4 cups [960 ml] sparkling water

2 cups [480 ml] freshly squeezed grapefruit juice (from 4 large grapefruits)

12 fl oz [360 ml] tequila

½ cup [120 ml] freshly squeezed lime juice (from 4 limes)

6 Tbsp [90 ml] freshly squeezed lemon juice (from 2 lemons)

Salt, for rimming the glasses

Lemon wedges, for garnish

Blueberries, for garnish

First, make the simple syrup. In a small saucepan over medium heat, combine the sugar, 1 cup [240 ml] of water, the blueberries, and lemon juice and bring to a boil. Lower the heat to medium and let simmer for 2 minutes, stirring often, until all the sugar has dissolved. Remove from the heat, stir in the lemon zest, and let cool. Once cooled, strain and discard the solids. The simple syrup can be made up to 1 week ahead of time and stored in an airtight container in the refrigerator.

To make the palomas, in a pitcher, combine the sparkling water, grapefruit juice, tequila, lime juice, lemon juice, and two-thirds of the simple syrup. Taste and add more simple syrup if you'd like it to be sweeter.

Pour a mound of salt onto a small dish that is slightly larger than your glasses and rub one of the lemon wedges around the rim of your glasses. Dip the rim of each glass in the salt mound.

Fill the salt-rimmed glasses with ice and pour in the paloma mixture. Garnish with lemon wedges and blueberries.

Raspberry Ginger Paloma Slushies

These are a bit more work than the big-batch options, but sometimes it's hot out and nothing else will do but an alcoholic slushie. Serve these to order to avoid them melting before guests can sip them down.

Serves 1

For the simple syrup

1 cup [200 g] sugar

1½ cups [180 g] fresh raspberries

1 in [2.5 cm] piece fresh ginger, peeled and roughly chopped

For the slushies

2 cups [280 g] crushed ice

⅓ cup [80 ml] grapefruit juice

2 fl oz [60 ml] tequila

2 Tbsp freshly squeezed lemon juice

Fresh raspberries or grapefruit wedge, for garnish

First, make the simple syrup. In a small saucepan over medium-high heat, combine the sugar, 1 cup [240 ml] of water, the raspberries, and ginger and bring to a boil. Lower the heat to medium and let simmer for 2 minutes, stirring often, until all the sugar has dissolved. Remove from the heat and let cool. Once cooled, strain and discard the solids.

To make the slushies, combine the ice, grapefruit juice, 3 Tbsp of the simple syrup, the tequila, and lemon juice in a blender. Blend on high speed for 2 minutes or until the ice has been crushed into a slushie texture. Transfer to a glass, top with a few fresh raspberries, and serve with a straw.

Section 2

Interactive
Spreads

SAVORY FOCACCIA PARTY

What's better than a pizza party? A focaccia party, of course! Start making the dough for this focaccia a few hours before your party so it's ready to go when your guests arrive.

Flavor Combination Ideas

rosemary + potato + apples + flaky sea salt + Fromage Fort (page 162)

sun-dried tomatoes + olives + lemon zest + red pepper flakes

½ Tbsp dollops of ricotta + chopped artichoke hearts + chopped thyme + Asiago cheese

torn kale + shredded Manchego + thinly sliced red onion

Styling Notes

Since this is an interactive spread, the styling is really going to be up to the guests as they add their own toppings to their section of the focaccia. Pick out some of your favorite pinch bowls and small shallow dishes to lay out the topping options. Place the toppings on the left side of the dough and the garnishes on the right side.

Spread Type

Assembly Spread

Drink Pairing

Keep with the Italian theme by serving up Aperol Spritz cocktails. To make one, combine 3 fl oz [90 ml] of Prosecco, 2 fl oz [60 ml] of Aperol, and 1 fl oz [30 ml] of soda water with ice in a wineglass. Garnish with an orange peel and enjoy!

Make-Ahead Game Plan

The Fromage Fort (page 162) can be made up to 3 days ahead of time and stored in an airtight container in the refrigerator. Components for the Greek-ish Salad with Orange-Fennel Vinaigrette (page 163) can be prepared the morning of and stored in individual containers in the refrigerator. Start preparing the focaccia dough 2½ hours before your guests arrive so it's on its second rise when they walk in. Prep all the toppings and garnishes 30 minutes before guests arrive. Dress the salad right before serving.

Wyatt's Sidebar

Adding torn pieces of salami over any of the flavor combinations after the focaccia has baked is a delicious way to amp up this spread.

Serves 8

1 batch focaccia dough (page 160)

2 cups [300 g] of any of the following
topping options:
thinly sliced apples,
thinly sliced Yukon gold potatoes,
halved cherry tomatoes,
minced garlic cloves,
crumbled goat cheese,
dollops of ricotta cheese,
sliced black or green olives,
sun-dried tomatoes,
artichoke hearts,
shredded Asiago or
Manchego cheese,
chopped rosemary or thyme leaves,
torn kale pieces,
thinly sliced red onion

Flaky sea salt

Olive oil, for drizzling

Greek-ish Salad with Orange-Fennel
Vinaigrette (page 163)

1 cup [150 g] garnish options: chopped
chives, chopped basil, pine nuts,
capers, red pepper flakes, lemon
zest, Fromage Fort (page 162)

Prepare the dough as instructed in the recipe (page 160). Preheat the oven to 425°F [220°C].

Place all the toppings into individual bowls and arrange on the table. Place all the garnish items into small bowls and set those off to the side.

Once the dough has doubled in size, press it down one last time with clean fingertips, leaving indents all over the dough. Place the sheet of dough on the table where you'll have your guests add their toppings.

Instruct your guests to sprinkle the dough with toppings, a large pinch of salt, and a drizzle of olive oil. Feel free to let guests pick their own sections to customize, or go wild as a team.

Bake for 20 to 25 minutes, or until the focaccia is golden brown on top. Meanwhile, remove the bowls of toppings from the table and replace them with a serving bowl of the Greek-ish Salad with Orange-Fennel Vinaigrette and all the bowls filled with garnish options.

When the focaccia is done, remove it from the oven and let cool before cutting into squares.

Let guests add garnishes to their individual squares of focaccia and enjoy!

Greek-ish
Salad

Focaccia Dough

This is my go-to recipe whenever I want to have some fresh bread for guests. Although this requires a little plan-ahead prep because of the rising times, this recipe is one of the easiest bread recipes I make.

Serves 8

2 cups [480 ml] warm water (around 110°F [43°C])

2¼ tsp active dry yeast

2 tsp sugar

5 cups [700 g] all-purpose flour

3 tsp fine sea salt

1 cup [240 ml] olive oil

Flaky sea salt, for finishing (optional)

Combine ¼ cup [60 ml] of the warm water, the yeast, and sugar in a small bowl and let sit for 10 minutes, or until bubbly.

In the bowl of a stand mixer fitted with the dough attachment, add the flour and fine sea salt and mix for a few seconds to combine. Add ½ cup [120 ml] of the olive oil, the remaining 1¾ cups [420 ml] of warm water, and the yeast mixture and knead on medium speed until the dough comes together, about 30 seconds. Turn the speed up to medium-high and knead for 5 minutes. Remove the dough, coat the mixing bowl in olive oil, and transfer the dough back to the oiled bowl. Cover with a clean dish towel and place in a warm location for 1 hour, or until doubled in size.

Drizzle the remaining ½ cup [120 ml] of olive oil into a half-sheet pan (18 by 13 in [46 by 33 cm])—this is going to look like a lot of oil but it'll produce a crispy crust. Transfer the dough into the prepared pan and use clean hands to press the dough into the pan. Turn the dough over to coat the other side with olive oil and continue to press the dough into the pan with your fingertips, making sure the dough stretches to fit the size of the pan. Cover and place in a warm spot until doubled in size, about 1 hour.

Continue with the instructions for baking the focaccia (see page 157). If you're not making the bread with the board of toppings and garnishes, sprinkle with the flaky sea salt before baking.

Fromage Fort

Surely I'm not the only one who ends up with all sorts of odds and ends of cheese in my cheese drawer? Once I've accumulate enough, I always make a batch of this Fromage Fort to use them up. (Both soft and hard cheeses will work just fine here!) Depending on how salty your cheese is, you may want to add a little salt at the end, so taste once it's ready and season as needed.

Serves 4 to 6 as a dip on its own or 8 as a topping component to smear on focaccia

---

8 oz [230 g] leftover cheese (ideally a mix of both soft and hard cheeses—feel free to clean out your fridge here!), cut into 1 in [2.5 cm] chunks

2 oz [55 g] cream cheese or unsalted butter

¼ cup [60 ml] dry white wine

1 garlic clove, minced

Freshly ground black pepper

½ tsp salt (optional)

Place the cheese, cream cheese, wine, and garlic in a food processor and process until completely smooth, about 30 seconds. Taste and season with pepper. Depending on how salty your cheese is, you may want to add a pinch of salt as well.

The Fromage Fort can be made up to 3 days ahead of time and stored in an airtight container in the refrigerator.

Greek-ish Salad with Orange-Fennel Vinaigrette

This salad reminds me of a fancier version of one we used to get at our local Greek pizzeria growing up. The fennel seeds really take the flavor of this salad to a new level, so make sure you don't skip them when making the dressing.

Serves 4 on its own or 8 as a side with the focaccia

For the quick-pickled onion

¼ cup [60 ml] red wine vinegar

⅛ tsp salt

1 small red onion, thinly sliced

For the dressing

1 tsp fennel seeds

3 Tbsp freshly squeezed orange juice (from about 1 medium orange)

Zest from 1 medium orange

1 Tbsp red wine vinegar

¼ tsp salt

⅛ tsp freshly ground black pepper

2 Tbsp olive oil

For the salad

1 head iceberg lettuce, rinsed and torn into bite-size pieces

1 cup [160 g] cherry tomatoes, halved

1 bell pepper (I like yellow for the pop of color), diced into 2 in [5 cm] pieces

4 oz [115 g] feta, broken up into bite-size pieces

To make the quick-pickled onion, in a small bowl, whisk together ¼ cup [60 ml] of water, the vinegar, and salt. Add the onion and set aside to pickle while preparing the rest of the salad.

To make the dressing, warm a small skillet over medium-low heat and add the fennel seeds. Let toast for 2 minutes, stirring often. Remove from the heat and roughly chop.

In a small bowl, whisk together the orange juice, orange zest, vinegar, fennel seeds, salt, and black pepper. While whisking, slowly pour in the olive oil until the dressing is emulsified. Set aside.

To make the salad, combine the lettuce, cherry tomatoes, and bell pepper in a large serving bowl. Drain the quick-pickled onions and add them to the bowl. Drizzle in the dressing and toss until the salad is completely coated with the dressing. Sprinkle the feta over the salad and serve.

LADIES' NIGHT LETTUCE WRAPS

Stop putting off getting together with your friends and schedule a hangout night NOW! You can make this spread, pull out that old Shania Twain CD (or Stevie Nicks or Hole or Beyoncé or whatever you all love to hang out to) and spend the evening eating, catching up, and laughing.

Make-Ahead Game Plan

The components for this spread are best made on the day of to keep them from getting soggy. You can make the Ginger Sesame Cauliflower filling (page **167**) and Crispy Quinoa (page **168**) earlier in the day and reheat before serving.

Flavor Combination Ideas

Use the Crispy Quinoa (page **168**) as a topping to add extra protein and crunch to your Ginger Sesame Cauliflower–filled wraps (page **167**).

Wyatt's Sidebar

Make an extra batch of the Ginger Sesame Cauliflower filling (page **167**) and substitute 1 lb [455 g] ground chicken for the cauliflower to give your guests an extra filling to choose from. To do this, add the chicken at the same time you would add the cauliflower but cook for 3 minutes, breaking up the chicken as it cooks, instead of the 2 minutes for cauliflower.

Drink Pairing

Serve with a sweet or off-dry white wine like a Riesling or Chenin Blanc to complement the spice in the wraps.

Spread Type

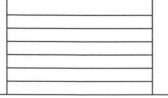

Assembly Spread or Statement Piece

Styling Notes

We've got two options for serving this one: Option one is that you can set everything up in a line on your grazing table that starts with the butter lettuce cups, followed by a bowl of filling, and then the individual bowls for the toppings so that your friends can customize it all themselves. Option two is to get some of the assembly prep done ahead of time by laying out the lettuce leaves onto a serving platter and distributing the filling evenly among them. This way your guests can pick up an already filled wrap and just add their desired toppings.

Serves 4 as a main or 6 to 8 as an appetizer/snack

2 heads butter lettuce, leaves washed and separated

1 batch Ginger Sesame Cauliflower (page 167)

1 batch Crispy Quinoa (page 168)

¼ cup [60 ml] tamari or soy sauce

¼ cup [60 ml] toasted sesame oil

2 Tbsp toasted sesame seeds

2 Tbsp red pepper flakes or chili garlic sauce

¼ cup [12 g] chopped green onions

¼ cup [10 g] chopped cilantro

8 lime wedges

For an assembly line: Place all of your ingredients into serving bowls. Working from left to right, put down your bowl of butter lettuce leaves, followed by the filling, and then all the bowls of toppings. Add tongs to the lettuce bowl and serving spoons to everything else.

Instruct your guests to start by grabbing a few lettuce leaves and piling in the filling followed by garnishing with whichever toppings they'd prefer.

For a platter display: Select a large serving platter that lets you lay out all of the lettuce leaves in a single layer. Divide the filling evenly between the lettuce cups.

Place the quinoa topping, tamari, sesame oil, sesame seeds, and red pepper flakes in small serving bowls and set them on top of the serving platter, leaving space between each bowl. Fill in the remaining space on the platter with the green onions, cilantro, and lime wedges.

Instruct your guests to grab a few filled lettuce cups and garnish them with whichever toppings they'd prefer.

Ginger Sesame Cauliflower

This veggie-packed filling comes together in only a few minutes and is a total crowd-pleaser! Don't skip on toasting the sesame seeds, as they add that much-needed crunch along with the Crispy Quinoa (page 168).

Serves 4 as a main or 6 to 8 as an appetizer/snack

---

3 tsp peanut or olive oil

1 head cauliflower, rinsed and chopped into small florets

½ cup [60 g] frozen peas

1 carrot, thinly sliced

3 Tbsp tamari or soy sauce

1 Tbsp tahini

1 Tbsp honey

2 tsp chili garlic sauce

1 tsp rice vinegar

1 garlic clove, minced

½ tsp grated fresh ginger

2 tsp freshly squeezed lime juice

1 Tbsp toasted sesame seeds

In a large skillet over medium heat, warm 1 tsp of the oil. Add the cauliflower florets and sauté for 2 minutes or just until the cauliflower is starting to soften slightly. Add ¼ cup [60 ml] of water, cover (leaving the lid slightly ajar to let steam escape), and let steam for 3 minutes. Add the peas and continue to steam for another 2 minutes or until the cauliflower is easily pierced with a fork. Uncover and sauté for 30 seconds or until most of the water has evaporated. Add the remaining 2 tsp of oil and the carrot and sauté for 5 minutes or until the carrot is beginning to brown.

Meanwhile, in a small mixing bowl, whisk together the tamari, tahini, honey, chili garlic sauce, rice vinegar, garlic, and ginger. Pour the mixture into the skillet and toss the vegetables around to get them completely coated in the sauce. Let cook, tossing the vegetables often, until the sauce has thickened and most of the moisture is cooked off, another 3 to 5 minutes.

Remove from the heat and add the lime juice. Top with the sesame seeds and serve right away.

Crispy Quinoa

Although I recommend using this as a topping on these lettuce wraps, this Crispy Quinoa is always great on top of salads and tacos too! Quinoa will crisp up after baking, so don't worry if it still has some moisture when you remove it from the oven.

Serves 8 as a topping

---

1 cup [180 g] quinoa, rinsed

¼ cup [60 ml] tamari or soy sauce

1 Tbsp olive oil

2 tsp chili garlic sauce

1 tsp rice vinegar

½ tsp ground ginger

In a medium saucepan over high heat, bring 2 cups [480 ml] of water to a boil. Once boiling, add the quinoa and lower the heat to low. Cover and let simmer for 15 minutes. Remove from the heat and let sit, covered, for an additional 10 minutes or until most of the liquid is absorbed. Fluff the quinoa with a fork.

Meanwhile, preheat the oven to 375°F [190°C] and line a baking sheet with parchment paper.

In a medium mixing bowl, whisk together the tamari, olive oil, chili garlic sauce, rice vinegar, and ginger.

Transfer the quinoa to the mixing bowl and stir until it's completely coated with the sauce.

Spread out the quinoa into an even layer on the prepared sheet. Bake for 25 to 35 minutes, stirring halfway through, until most of the quinoa has browned and the quinoa no longer feels wet.

Remove from the oven and let cool before serving.

Crispy Quinoa

FALAFEL MEZZE SPREAD

I love how the pan-fried falafel makes this hearty enough for a meal. Everything else in this spread is rather light, so it's a perfect choice for summer gatherings when you're looking for something tasty to fill you up but not weigh you down.

Make-Ahead Game Plan

The falafel patties (page 175) are best served fresh but can be made up to 3 days ahead of time and reheated in the oven. The Baba Ghanoush (page 176) can also be made up to 3 days ahead of time and stored in an airtight container in the refrigerator; let it come to room temperature when serving and wait to top with the Fried Walnuts & Pomegranate Seeds until right before serving. The day before, make the Israeli Couscous with Mint-Parsley Oil (page 179) and chop the vegetables; store the veggies in airtight containers in the refrigerator (spritz them with water before serving if they look dry). Assemble the spread 30 minutes before guests arrive while you are reheating the falafel.

Spread Type

Statement Piece or Abundance Spread

Wyatt's Sidebar

If you're feeling up for the challenge of planning ahead, add spiced chicken kebabs to this spread by threading 2 lb [910 g] boneless chicken thighs, cut into bite-size pieces, onto metal skewers. Make a yogurt marinade with 1 cup [240 g] Greek yogurt, 2 Tbsp olive oil, ½ tsp cumin, ½ tsp smoked paprika, and 1 tsp salt. Spoon the marinade over the skewers, cover, and let sit overnight. When ready to serve, grill the kebabs over medium-high heat for 10 to 15 minutes, flipping halfway through, or until cooked through. Finish with a squeeze of lemon juice.

Styling Notes

Start out by plating the Pan-Fried Falafel Patties (page 175), Baba Ghanoush (page 176), and Israeli Couscous with Mint-Parsley Oil (page 179) on a nice platter and then fan out all the extra condiments and dipping options around them. You'll want to make sure anything that might spread (like the yogurt) is in its own bowl and that you have the correct-size platter to fill it fully with food.

Drink Pairing

Make a batch of refreshing Middle Eastern limonana: In a blender, blend 1 cup [240 ml] freshly squeezed lemon juice, 2 cups [24 g] loosely packed mint leaves, and ¾ cup [150 g] sugar. Strain the liquid into a pitcher with 4 cups [960 ml] of water and serve over ice.

Serves 4 as a main or 6 as an appetizer

1 batch Pan-Fried Falafel Patties
(page 175)

1 batch Baba Ghanoush with Fried
Walnuts & Pomegranate Seeds
(page 176)

1 batch Israeli Couscous with Mint-
Parsley Oil (page 179)

1 cup [240 g] Greek yogurt

3 Tbsp fresh dill

1 Tbsp olive oil

3 tsp za'atar

6 pieces pita, cut into triangles

1 cup [160 g] cherry tomatoes, halved

½ cup [70 g] sliced carrots

½ cup [75 g] sliced cucumbers

½ small red onion, thinly sliced

¼ cup [55 g] roasted red peppers

¼ cup [10 g] chopped cilantro

1 cup [120 g] crumbled feta cheese

Salt and freshly ground black pepper

Place a large serving board or platter on your grazing table. Arrange the Pan-Fried Falafel Patties neatly on a small serving plate and place it in the middle of the serving board. Transfer the Baba Ghanoush and Israeli Couscous to serving bowls and add them to the serving board.

In a small mixing bowl, stir together the Greek yogurt and 1 Tbsp of the dill. Drizzle with the olive oil and 1 tsp of the za'atar. Place the remaining za'atar in a small serving bowl and add both bowls to the serving board. Arrange the pita, tomatoes, carrots, cucumbers, red onions, roasted red peppers, cilantro, feta, and remaining 2 Tbsp of dill around the serving board, using up any remaining space. Add a dish of salt and pepper to the side of the board and serve.

Pan-Fried Falafel Patties

This pan-fried version makes re-creating falafel in your home kitchen easier than ever (because, let's be real, how many of us really like to deep-fry things at home?). I also rely on canned chickpeas instead of dried so these can come together in minutes instead of days.

Serves 4 as a main or 6 to 8 as an appetizer

Two 15 oz [430 g] cans chickpeas, drained and rinsed

6 garlic cloves, minced

½ cup [24 g] chopped green onions

¼ cup [10 g] chopped cilantro

¼ cup [10 g] chopped parsley leaves

2 tsp salt

2 tsp coriander

2 tsp cumin

2 tsp baking powder

¼ tsp cayenne pepper

¼ tsp freshly ground black pepper

¼ to ⅓ cup [35 to 45 g] all-purpose flour

Vegetable oil, for frying

In a food processor fitted with the blade attachment, add the chickpeas, garlic, green onions, cilantro, parsley, salt, coriander, cumin, baking powder, cayenne pepper, and black pepper. Pulse until a coarse meal has formed, about 20 pulses. Sprinkle in ¼ cup [35 g] of the flour and pulse another 5 times or until incorporated. Squeeze a dime-size amount of the the dough between your fingers to see if it sticks together. If it doesn't, add more flour, 1 Tbsp at a time, until it does (up to ⅓ cup [45 g] total). Cover and let chill in the refrigerator for at least 15 minutes.

Use clean hands to form 2 by ½ in [5 cm by 12 mm] round patties (you should end up with a total of 20 patties).

Line a plate with two layers of paper towels. In a small 8 in [20 cm] skillet over medium heat, warm ¾ in [2 cm] of vegetable oil. You'll know the oil is ready when a drop of water sizzles in the skillet.

Fry the falafel patties, four at a time, until golden brown on both sides, 2 to 3 minutes per side. Use a slotted spoon to transfer the falafels to the prepared plate and repeat with the rest of the falafels. Serve right away.

The falafel is best served fresh but can be made up to 3 days ahead of time and reheated in the oven.

Baba Ghanoush with Fried Walnuts & Pomegranate Seeds

This dip is a real showstopper with the walnut topping and pomegranate seeds! If pomegranate seeds aren't in season, you could top with raisins instead.

Serves 4 to 6

For the baba ghanoush

1 large eggplant

3 Tbsp tahini

2 Tbsp freshly squeezed lemon juice

1 garlic clove, minced

1 Tbsp parsley

¼ tsp salt

¼ tsp cumin

2 Tbsp olive oil

For the topping

2 Tbsp olive oil

¼ cup [30 g] chopped walnuts

⅛ tsp salt

¼ cup [50 g] pomegranate seeds, for garnish

1 Tbsp torn parsley leaves, for garnish

Pita chips or pita slices, for serving

Preheat the oven to 450°F [230°C] and line a baking sheet with aluminum foil.

To make the baba ganoush, poke the eggplant all over with a fork to speed up the cooking process and put it on the prepared baking sheet. Bake for 30 minutes or until the eggplant is easily pierced with a knife. Remove from the oven and let cool.

Once cool enough to handle, slice the eggplant in half and scrape out the insides into a food processor fitted with the blade attachment. Add the tahini, lemon juice, garlic, parsley, salt, and cumin. Process until smooth, about 30 seconds. With the motor running, pour in the olive oil and process for another 30 seconds or until light and fluffy. Transfer the dip to a serving bowl.

To make the topping, in a small saucepan over medium heat, warm the olive oil. Add the walnuts and, tossing often, cook for 2 minutes or until they start to turn dark brown. Remove from the heat and sprinkle in the salt. Spoon the walnuts over the dip and pour any remaining olive oil from the saucepan over the top. Garnish with the pomegranate seeds and parsley. Serve warm or at room temperature.

This can be made up to 3 days ahead of time and stored in an airtight container in the refrigerator—let it come to room temperature when serving and wait to top with the fried walnuts and pomegranate seeds until right before serving. Serve with pita chips.

Israeli Couscous with Mint-Parsley Oil

Make sure to use Israeli couscous (also called pearl couscous) in this recipe. It's a large couscous that should not be confused with Moroccan couscous, which has a completely different cooking time.

Serves 6 to 8

---

2 cups [280 g] dried Isreaeli couscous

¼ tsp salt, plus more for seasoning the water

1 cup [12 g] fresh herbs (such as parsley, mint, chives, etc.)

¾ cup [180 ml] olive oil

1 cup [160 g] cherry tomatoes, halved

3 green onions, thinly sliced

2 Tbsp freshly squeezed lemon juice

Zest from 1 lemon

2 Tbsp chopped mint

2 Tbsp chopped parsley

Freshly ground black pepper

In a small saucepan over high heat, bring 2¼ cups [540 ml] of water to a boil. Add the couscous, lower the heat to low to maintain a simmer, and cover. Let cook for 8 to 10 minutes, stirring often, until all the water is absorbed and the couscous is soft. Remove from the heat and set aside.

Meanwhile, in a medium saucepan over high heat, bring 4 cups [960 ml] of salted water to a boil. Place some ice and water in a medium mixing bowl and set aside to create an ice bath. Once the salted water is boiling, add in the fresh herbs and blanch for 20 seconds or until the herbs are bright green. Use tongs to transfer the blanched herbs to the ice bath for 1 minute, then transfer the herbs to a paper towel to remove excess water.

Place the blanched herbs in a high speed blender with the olive oil and blend until combined, about 30 seconds. Place a fine-mesh sieve over a small bowl and strain the herb oil through the sieve; discard the solids.

In a medium mixing bowl, stir together the cooked couscous, ½ cup [120 ml] of the herb oil (reserve the rest for serving in case your guests would like to add more), the cherry tomatoes, green onions, lemon juice, lemon zest, mint, parsley, and the salt. Toss until completely coated, then let sit for at least 30 minutes to let the flavors develop. Taste and season with salt and pepper.

Serve right away or transfer to an airtight container and store in the refrigerator for up to 2 days.

PIEROGI DUMPLING PARTY

Maybe it's the socially awkward introvert in me, but I love bringing people together to do more than sit around and chat. This is exactly why I love hosting cooking nights where I invite friends over to create a meal; it's a way to spend time together while also working toward creating something delicious.

I find that this spread works best if you plan ahead and make the filling before everyone arrives so you can jump right into stuffing the dumplings together. I also like to designate one person to be in charge of dough (since they will probably have to make and roll it out in batches) and boiling the pierogi while everyone else is in charge of stuffing the pierogi. If you happen to have a pierogi press, then you are already ahead of the game and can use it to stuff several pierogi at the same time. If you don't, fear not because you can easily use a 3 in [7.5 cm] biscuit cutter or the rim of a water glass.

Depending on how precise your team of stuffers is, you may end up with extra filling—feel free to either make more dough and keep going (pierogi freeze beautifully!) or save the filling for another use. Keep the dough covered when not in use.

Styling Notes

Worry less about the presentation on this one and more about creating a seamless assembly process for your friends so the night can be stress-free and delicious!

When it is time to eat, serve the pierogi family style with all the garnishes laid out in their own nice serving bowls spread out on the table.

Wyatt's Sidebar

When getting ready to cook the pierogi, slice up big chunks of bratwurst (or Italian sausage) and panfry them in the butter until almost cooked through before adding the pierogi to brown up with them.

Spread Type

Assembly Spread

Drink Pairing

Make an easy big-batch white wine spritzer with two 750 ml bottles of white wine (such as Riesling, Sauvignon Blanc, etc.), 2 cups [480 ml] of club soda, a dash of citrus bitters, and lemon twists for garnish.

Make-Ahead Game Plan

Fillings can be made the day before and stored in airtight containers in the refrigerator.

Serves 12 to 15

1 batch Potato–Sour Cream Filling (page 188) or Spinach-Feta Filling (page 186)

1 batch Spiced Plum Cheesecake Filling (page 187)

1 batch Basic Pierogi Dough (page 183)

Salt and freshly ground black pepper

10 Tbsp [140 g] unsalted butter or olive oil

2 bell peppers, any color, sliced

2 red onions, sliced

Parsley, for garnish

½ cup [120 g] sour cream

1 batch Radicchio Salad (page 190)

1 cup [85 g] crushed graham crackers, for garnish

Place 1 cup [240 ml] of water to the side of your workstation. Put all the fillings in their own bowls and add 1 tsp to each bowl. Divide the dough into five equal pieces.

To assemble with a pierogi press: Working with two pieces of dough at a time, roll the dough into two rectangles that are each about ⅛ in [4 mm] thick. Lay one dough piece over the press and fill each indentation with 1 to 1½ tsp of one of the fillings. Dip a clean finger or a pastry brush into the water and run it along the edge of the dough. Place the other dough rectangle directly over the top and roll a rolling pin over the dough to seal. Turn the press over so the pierogi fall out, removing any excess dough. Transfer to a floured baking sheet. Repeat with the remaining filling and dough (rerolling dough scraps as needed).

To assemble by hand: Working with one piece of dough at a time, roll the dough into a rectangle that's about ⅛ in [4 mm] thick. Use the rim of a 3 in [7.5 cm] glass or biscuit cutter to cut out about 10 rounds. Place 1 to 1½ tsp of filling in the center of each round, then dip a clean finger or a pastry brush into the water and run it along the edge of the dough. Fold the dough over to form a half-moon and use a fork to press the edges together. Transfer to a floured baking sheet. Repeat with the remaining filling and dough (rerolling dough scraps as needed).

Bring a large pot of salted water to a boil over high heat. Working in batches, add enough pierogi to fit in a single layer and boil until they float, 4 to 5 minutes. Remove with a slotted spoon and set aside

In a large nonstick skillet over medium heat, melt 1 Tbsp of butter. Working in batches, toss in enough pierogi to fit in a single layer. Cook, stirring often, until they are brown on all sides, 7 to 10 minutes. Repeat with the remaining pierogi, adding 1 Tbsp more of the butter per batch.

Heat 2 Tbsp of the butter in a large nonstick skillet and add the bell peppers and onions. Sauté for 7 to 10 minute or until softened. Remove from the heat and season with salt and pepper.

Place the pierogi on three serving trays (grouped by filling), garnish the savory pierogi with parsley, and set the trays on the table. Transfer the sautéed onions and peppers, sour cream, and Radicchio Salad to their own serving bowls and place on the table. Transfer the crushed graham crackers to a serving bowl and set near the sweet pierogi serving tray. Add serving utensils to each of the bowls and serve right away.

Basic Pierogi Dough

This recipe yields enough dough for six dozen pierogi, which sounds like a lot (and it is!) but you would be surprised at how quickly these will go once people start eating them. Plus, making pierogi is a bit of a process, so I always recommend making a big batch and freezing some for later. To freeze, boil the stuffed pierogi. Cool completely, then wrap in parchment paper and place in a freezer-safe resealable plastic bag. Pierogis keep, frozen, up to 3 months. If you still don't think you need that many pierogi in your life, this recipe can easily be halved.

If you have a food processor with a volume of 11 cups or less, I recommend making the dough in two batches.

Yields about 6 dozen pierogi

---

6 cups [840 g] all-purpose flour, plus more as needed

1 cup [240 ml] whole milk, plus more as needed

¾ cup [165 g] cold unsalted butter, cut into cubes

2 eggs

½ Tbsp fine sea salt

In a food processor, combine the flour, milk, butter, eggs, and salt and pulse until well combined, about 30 seconds. Add more flour, 1 Tbsp at a time, if the dough is too sticky. Add more milk, 1 Tbsp at a time, if the dough is too crumbly.

Transfer the dough to a floured surface and divide it into four equal pieces. Wrap the dough pieces in a damp kitchen towel and set aside until ready to roll out.

Spinach-Feta Filling

I tested a lot of filling variations, and this "spanakopita" filling was always a clear winner. The salty feta really punches through the other flavors, while the ricotta gives it a creamy texture.

Yields 2½ cups [545 g]

1 Tbsp olive oil

2 garlic cloves, minced

5 oz [140 g] fresh spinach, roughly chopped

8 oz [230 g] feta, crumbled

8 oz [230 g] ricotta

2 Tbsp whole milk

⅛ tsp freshly ground black pepper

In a medium skillet over medium heat, warm the oil. Add the garlic and sauté for 30 seconds or until just starting to turn brown and fragrant. Add the spinach and cook for 2 to 3 minutes, tossing often, or just until all the spinach has wilted. Remove from the heat and let cool.

Meanwhile, in a large bowl, whisk together the feta, ricotta, milk, and pepper until combined.

Once the spinach has cooled, remove any excess liquid by wrapping the spinach in a clean dish cloth and wringing it out over the sink. Transfer the spinach to the feta mixture and stir until evenly incorporated.

Spiced Plum Cheesecake Filling

I couldn't not include a sweet pierogi option! I created this filling after making several cheesecakes for Wyatt's birthday (they are his favorite) and wondering, Can you stuff this into a pierogi? Turns out you can! I love using plum preserve around the holidays but have also made this with strawberry spread in the summer—just make sure whatever spread you use, it has a smooth consistency so you don't end up with chunks in your filling. Try garnishing with crumbled graham crackers.

Using a stand mixer fitted with the paddle attachment on medium-high speed, beat together the cream cheese, plum preserve, sour cream, confectioners' sugar, vanilla, salt, cinnamon, nutmeg, and ginger until light and fluffy, 2 to 3 minutes. Lower the speed to medium and slowly pour in the heavy cream until incorporated. Turn the speed back up to medium-high and beat for another 1 to 2 minutes or until light and fluffy.

Yields about 2½ cups [550 g]

---

1 lb [455 g] cream cheese, at room temperature

½ cup [150 g] plum preserve or fruit spread

¼ cup [60 g] sour cream

¼ cup [30 g] confectioners' sugar

½ tsp vanilla extract

½ tsp salt

½ tsp ground cinnamon

¼ tsp ground nutmeg

¼ tsp ground ginger

¼ cup [60 ml] heavy cream, at room temperature

Potato–Sour Cream Filling

Potato is the traditional filling I grew up with as a kid. We've adjusted the recipe since then (we used to use russet potatoes and no sour cream), so this current version is the product of years of testing. If you have my first cookbook, *Vegetarian Heartland*, you'll notice that this recipe has evolved quite a bit in just the few short years between these two books. Will it continue to evolve? You'll have to pick up my sixth book in 2030 to find out. (Jk! No confirmed fourth . . . or fifth . . . or sixth book . . . YET—I was just trying to be cheeky. Did it work?)

Yields about 3 cups [690 g]

⅛ tsp salt, plus more for seasoning the water

1½ lb [680 g] Yukon gold potatoes, peeled and finely diced

½ cup [40 g] shredded Cheddar cheese

¼ cup [60 g] sour cream

2 Tbsp unsalted butter

Bring a large pot of salted water to a boil over high heat. Add the potatoes and boil until they are easily pierced with a fork, about 10 minutes. Drain the potatoes and transfer to a large bowl. Use a potato masher to mash the potatoes until mostly smooth. Fold in the cheese, sour cream, butter (the heat from the potatoes will melt the ingredients as you mix), and salt until combined.

Potato–Sour
Cream Filling

Radicchio Salad

This bright and bitter salad is a delicious contrast to the Polish dumplings. I prefer to just give the radicchio a quick rinse. If you find radicchio too bitter, you can soak the leaves in water for up to 30 minutes to tame it a bit, but you will lose some of the crunch.

Serves 8

¼ cup [60 ml] olive oil

1 Tbsp honey

1 Tbsp white wine vinegar

½ tsp salt, plus more for seasoning

½ tsp freshly ground black pepper, plus more for seasoning

2 heads radicchio, cored and chopped into 1 in [2.5 cm] pieces

2 oz [55 g] Manchego cheese, thinly sliced

1 cup [140 g] pitted and halved green olives

In a small bowl, whisk together the olive oil, honey, vinegar, salt, and pepper until incorporated.

In a large serving bowl, add the radicchio, cheese, and olives. Drizzle in the dressing and toss to coat. Taste and season with more salt and pepper, if needed.

BOOZY BLOODY MARY BAR

Hands down my favorite part about brunch is the Bloody Mary, so I love to create this spread for family holidays and when friends come to visit and spend the night. This board also goes great with both the Creamy Polenta Spread (page 132) and Christmas Morning Dutch Baby Party (page 262).

Make-Ahead Game Plan

Bloody Mary and rim salt mixes can be made up to 3 days before (wait to add liquor and ice until right before serving). Store the Bloody Mary mixes in airtight containers in the refrigerator and salt rim mixes in airtight containers at room temperature. Citrus wedges can be sliced the morning of, and the spread can be assembled up to 30 minutes before serving (except for the ice).

Spread Type

Drink Station

Wyatt's Sidebar

Serve cooked shrimp on the garnish table as an extra option for your guests to add to their serving skewers.

Drink Pairing

Depending on your alcohol of choice, feel free to swap out the vodka for tequila (a Bloody Maria), gin (a Red Snapper), or skip the alcohol completely for a virgin twist.

Styling Notes

I like to style the garnishes like they are their own cheese board, with piles of ingredients spread out over a wood or marble board. Alternatively, you could put all the garnish ingredients into their own separate serving bowls and scatter them on the counter near the Bloody Mary pitchers. Place toothpick spears in a small glass and add it to the serving area.

Also, I don't like horseradish in my Bloody Marys (and I KNOW I'm not the only one!), so I keep it on the side along with the hot sauce so folks can add it to their taste.

Flavor Combination Ideas

Quick Harissa Bloody Mary Mix (page 197) + Za'atar Rim Salt (page 201) + lemon wedge + celery stalk + pickled veggies + hot sauce

Smoky Carrot Bloody Mary Mix (page 198) + Smoky Rim Salt (page 201) + lime wedge + pickle spear + cheese-stuffed olives

Serves 16

1 batch **Quick Harissa Bloody Mary Mix** (page 197)

1 batch **Smoky Carrot Bloody Mary Mix** (page 198)

1 batch **Za'atar Rim Salt** (page 201)

1 batch **Smoky Rim Salt** (page 201)

8 lemon wedges

8 lime wedges

8 pickle spears

16 cheese-stuffed olives

2 cups [480 g] pickled and/or marinated vegetables (such as marinated pearl onions, pepperoncinis, artichoke hearts, carrots, asparagus, cornichons, etc.)

8 celery stalks

1½ cups [120 g] cubed Cheddar cheese

Fresh dill, for garnish

Hot sauce and horseradish, for serving (optional, but recommended so people can add more spice if they'd like)

Transfer the Bloody Mary mixes to pitchers and place them on your serving area. Spread out the rim salts into shallow dishes and add them to the serving area. Put down a wood or marble serving board and pile the citrus wedges onto the board. Anything that could spread or has liquid (such as the pickles and olives) should be put into small serving dishes and added to the serving board. Fill in the remaining space with celery stalks, Cheddar, and fresh dill. Transfer the hot sauce and horseradish, if using, to small serving bowls and place them next to the board. Add serving utensils to the board and serve.

Quick Harissa Bloody Mary Mix

What makes this mix unique is leaning into the hot harissa sauce (which is a Tunisian red pepper sauce) for the heat and A.1. sauce (yes–the steak sauce!) for a punch of umami flavor.

Serves 8

---

4 cups [960 ml] tomato juice

8 fl oz [240 ml] vodka

3 Tbsp hot harissa sauce

3 Tbsp freshly squeezed lemon juice

2 Tbsp A.1. sauce

1 Tbsp freshly squeezed lime juice

2 tsp celery salt

½ tsp freshly ground black pepper

½ tsp salt

Transfer all the ingredients into a large pitcher and stir. Cover and refrigerate for at least 1 hour.

Serve chilled with ice.

The mix can be made up to 3 days ahead (but wait to add the vodka and ice until right before serving). Store in an airtight container in the refrigerator.

Smoky Carrot Bloody Mary Mix

Want to really surprise your guests with a new twist on the Bloody Mary? Make this smoky carrot version! This version uses carrot juice instead of tomato, which can be found in the juice aisle.

Serves 8

---

4 cups [960 ml] carrot juice

8 fl oz [240 ml] vodka

2 Tbsp sriracha or your favorite hot sauce

1 tsp freshly squeezed lemon juice

2 tsp celery salt

½ tsp salt

½ tsp freshly ground black pepper

Transfer all of the ingredients into a large pitcher and stir. Cover and refrigerate for at least 1 hour.

Serve chilled with ice.

The mix can be made up to 3 days ahead (but wait to add the vodka and ice until right before serving). Store in an airtight container in the refrigerator.

Smoky Carrot

Za'atar Rim Salt

Both of these salts work great for either Bloody Mary recipe!

Yields 4½ Tbsp [44 g], enough for 8 to 10 glasses

2 Tbsp flaky sea salt or kosher salt

1 Tbsp dried oregano

1 Tbsp fresh or dried thyme leaves

1½ tsp sumac

Lemon or lime wedge

In a small mixing bowl, combine the salt, oregano, thyme, and sumac. Transfer the mixture to a shallow saucer. Rub a lemon or lime wedge along the rim of a glass and roll the rim in the salt mixture until the rim is completely coated. Repeat as needed with additional glasses.

Store this salt in an airtight container at room temperature and use within 3 months for best flavor.

Smoky Rim Salt

Yields ¼ cup [55 g], enough for 8 to 10 glasses

2 Tbsp flaky sea salt or kosher salt

1 Tbsp smoked paprika

1 Tbsp celery salt

¾ tsp ground mustard

Lemon or lime wedge

In a small mixing bowl, combine the salt, paprika, celery salt, and ground mustard. Transfer the mixture to a shallow saucer. Rub a lemon or lime wedge along the rim of a glass and roll the rim in the salt mixture until the rim is completely coated. Repeat as needed with additional glasses.

Store this salt in an airtight container at room temperature and use within 3 months for best flavor.

Section 3

Holiday
Showstoppers

BIRTHDAY BREAKFAST NACHO BUFFET

This is for all my friends who like to be in bed by 10 p.m. (hiii—that is me!) and would prefer to celebrate during the day. The recipes in this spread easily serve six to eight people, which is perfect if you're hosting a small gathering. But this is also a very easy board to double or triple, depending on how many guests you plan to have over.

Spread Type

Buffet Style or Family Style

Styling Notes

I like to serve the nachos on a baking sheet so there is more surface area for the toppings. Pile your stack of tortilla chips high with toppings and then place additional toppings to the side in small bowls so guests can heap on even more if they'd like.

Drink Pairing

Either of the big-batch paloma recipes on pages 150 to 151 would work great with this spread if you are into a little morning drinking (it is someone's birthday, after all!). A great nonalcoholic option would be a batch of limeade like the recipe on page 240.

Wyatt's Sidebar

Make seasoned ground beef as a topping option! Brown up 1 lb [455 g] of ground beef over medium-high heat in a large skillet for 8 to 10 minutes. Drain any excess fat and season the beef with your favorite taco spices (such as cumin, garlic powder, smoked paprika, and chili powder).

Flavor Combination Ideas

Why limit yourself when you could make 'em extra loaded and pile everything on for the perfect nacho?!

Make-Ahead Game Plan

The Poblano & Pepita Verde Sauce (page 211) can be made the night before and stored in an airtight container in the refrigerator. Plan to block off the hour before guests arrive to transfer all the topping options to bowls, make the Loaded Guacamole (page 209), melt the cheese on the tortilla chips, and make the Sour Cream & Chive Scrambled Eggs (page 208). Scrambled eggs get cold surprisingly quickly, so after cooking, consider keeping them in a slow cooker set to low heat and placed on the grazing table to keep warm if guests aren't digging in right away.

Serves 6 to 8

1 batch **Loaded Guacamole** (page 209)

1 batch **Poblano & Pepita Verde Sauce** (page 211)

1 head **iceberg lettuce, trimmed and shredded**

2 cups [320 g] **cherry tomatoes, halved**

1½ cups [240 g] **warmed black beans (I use canned beans)**

1½ cups [360 g] **salsa (choose a medium heat unless you know all your guests' preferred spice levels)**

1 cup [240 g] **sour cream**

1 cup [160 g] **black olives, pitted and quartered**

½ bunch **radishes, stems removed and thinly sliced**

½ cup [60 g] **pickled jalapeños**

¼ cup [12 g] **chopped green onions or chives**

¼ cup [10 g] **chopped cilantro**

One 13 oz [370 g] **bag tortilla chips**

2 cups [160 g] **shredded Cheddar cheese**

1 batch **Sour Cream & Chive Scrambled Eggs** (page 208)

Transfer the Loaded Guacamole, Poblano & Pepita Verde Sauce, shredded lettuce, cherry tomatoes, beans, salsa, sour cream, olives, radishes, jalapeños, green onions, and cilantro into individual serving bowls and place them on your grazing table. Add serving spoons to each bowl.

Right before your guests arrive, place an oven rack in the top third of the oven and preheat the broiler. Spread out half of the tortilla chips onto a large baking sheet and sprinkle 1 cup [80 g] of the cheese over the chips. Add another layer by topping the cheese with the remaining chips and the remaining 1 cup [80 g] of cheese. Place the baking sheet in the oven and cook until the cheese has melted, 2 to 4 minutes, watching closely to make sure the chips don't burn. Transfer the baking sheet to your grazing table.

Make the Sour Cream & Chive Scrambled Eggs right before serving. Place the warm eggs on a serving plate and arrange it near the topping bowls on the grazing table.

Loaded Guac

Sour Cream & Chive Scrambled Eggs

The addition of sour cream really gives these scrambled eggs a creamy end result. When mixing everything together, it's okay if the sour cream doesn't mix completely into the rest of the ingredients—a few pockets of sour cream in your eggs will only add to the velvety end result.

Serves 3 as a main or 6 to 8 as an appetizer

---

6 eggs

6 Tbsp [100 g] sour cream

½ tsp salt

Dash of freshly ground black pepper

2 Tbsp unsalted butter

1 Tbsp chopped chives

In a small mixing bowl, whisk together the eggs, sour cream, salt, and pepper.

In a large nonstick skillet over medium heat, melt the butter. Once the butter starts to bubble, add the egg mixture. Watch the eggs closely until the edges start to set, 15 to 30 seconds. Lower the heat to medium-low and use a spatula or wooden spoon to make large sweeps across the bottom of the skillet to create large curds. Continue to do this until the eggs are almost set (don't let them dry out completely, as they'll continue to cook slightly off the heat), 4 to 6 minutes. Remove from the heat and fold in the chives.

Loaded Guacamole

Wyatt's mom often makes a version of this when she and Wyatt's dad come visit in the summer. I love how you not only get an extra serving of veggies, but also that the addition brings a welcome crunch to the guacamole.

Serves 6 to 8

---

4 ripe avocados, halved and pitted

3 tsp freshly squeezed lime juice, plus more as needed

½ tsp hot sauce

½ tsp salt, plus more as needed

¼ tsp cumin

¼ tsp garlic powder

¼ tsp freshly ground black pepper

1 Roma tomato, cored and diced

½ bell pepper, diced

2 Tbsp finely diced red onion

1 Tbsp chopped cilantro

Scoop out the avocado flesh into a medium bowl along with the lime juice, hot sauce, salt, cumin, garlic powder, and black pepper. Use a fork to smash the spices into the avocado until evenly distributed. Fold in the tomato, bell pepper, onion, and cilantro. Taste and adjust the seasoning if needed (it will most likely need either more salt or lime juice). Serve right away.

Poblano & Pepita Verde Sauce

Use this no-cook sauce as a finishing touch to add an irresistible brightness to dishes such as nachos, tacos, and even salads!

Yields 1½ cups [320 g]

½ cup [120 ml] red wine vinegar

¼ cup [30 g] finely chopped poblano pepper

2 Tbsp finely diced red onion

4 garlic cloves, finely chopped

1 tsp salt

¼ cup [35 g] roasted pepitas (unsalted)

1 Tbsp chopped chives

½ cup [120 ml] olive oil

In a small mixing bowl, stir together the vinegar, poblano, onion, garlic, and salt and let sit for 10 minutes. Stir in the pepitas and chives. Slowly stream in the olive oil while whisking the mixture until emulsified.

PUPPY BOWL (SUPER BOWL) CRUDITÉS & DIPS SPREAD

Anyone who knows me knows I'm not the kind of person to watch the Super Bowl when an adorable yearly tradition like the Puppy Bowl is on TV at the same time (google "Puppy Bowl starting lineup" if you don't know what I'm talking about—you won't be disappointed by the puppy pics you will be blessed with). However, in an attempt to be more inclusive of everyone, I'm giving this spread a dual name because I've been told it's a great option for entertaining during either event.

Think of this spread as an elevated homemade veggie tray that goes way beyond store-bought ranch dressing and pre-cut vegetables. Also, if you can't tell by looking at the dips in this spread, my favorite way to get friends and family (read: Wyatt) to eat veggies is to involve cheese—lots and lots of cheese.

Make-Ahead Game Plan

The Homemade Ricotta (page 220) can be made 2 days ahead of time (wait to top it with the additional dip items until right before serving). The Caramelized Shallot Jam Dip (page 218) and Baked Artichoke–Smoked Gouda Spread (page 217) can be made the day before (wait to broil until right before serving) and stored, covered, in the refrigerator. The vegetables can also be chopped the day before and stored in an airtight container in the refrigerator. Broil the Baked Artichoke–Smoked Gouda Dip and make the Warmed Tomatoes, Olives & Spicy Honey (page 220) 30 minutes before serving. Assemble the entire spread 15 minutes before guests arrive.

Spread Type

Abundance Spread

_____

_____

_____

_____

_____

_____

_____

Styling Notes

I like to pile this one high since it's for a casual event and it means I won't have to add more food to the board throughout the game. Make piles and stack each type of veggie in its own area rather than mixing them all together to keep from making the spread look too busy.

Are your veggies starting to look a little sad halfway through the game? Keep a clean spray bottle filled with water nearby and spritz the veggies to bring them back to life. Feeling weird about spritzing in front of friends? Get new friends (joking, obviously!) or wait to put the veggies out until the last possible minute and spritz them right before guests arrive so they start out as hydrated as possible.

Serves 12

1 batch Baked Artichoke–Smoked Gouda Spread (page 217)

1 batch Caramelized Shallot Jam Dip (page 218)

1 batch Homemade Ricotta with Warmed Tomatoes, Olives & Spicy Honey (page 220)

6 cups [960 g] vegetables, washed and chopped into bite-size pieces (such as carrots, radishes, broccoli, cauliflower, tomatoes, beets, radicchio, etc.)

2 cups [170 g] crackers or potato chips

Transfer the prepared dips in their serving bowls onto one or two large serving platters, depending on what size platter you have. Fill in the platters with the vegetables, splitting up piles of similar-colored and shaped vegetables so they aren't next to each other.

Place the crackers in a serving bowl and set it next to the crudités platter.

Wyatt's Sidebar

With Shelly doing all the dip and veggie prep in the kitchen, I like to stay out of the way by picking up an order of buffalo wings from either our local grocery or a local wing joint.

Drink Pairing

Pair this board with a light beer, because I've heard beer is always supposed to be involved when watching sports.

Flavor Combination Ideas

All the veggies should work well with all the dips, but if I have to pick favorites:

Caramelized Shallot Jam Dip (page 218) + carrots

Baked Artichoke–Smoked Gouda Spread (page 217) + radicchio cups

Homemade Ricotta with Warmed Tomatoes, Olives & Spicy Honey (page 220) + crackers

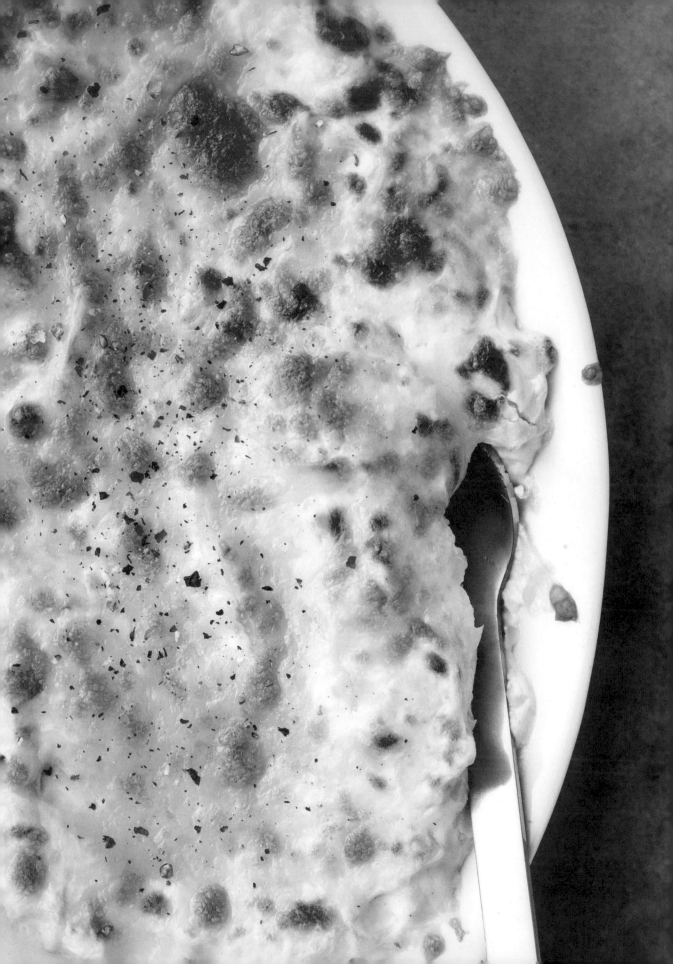

Baked Artichoke–Smoked Gouda Spread

Inspired by my favorite cream cheese flavor offered at our local bagel bakery, this very cheesy dip is incredible when warm and gooey. Make sure to use smoked Gouda in this recipe, as the smokiness gives this dip its flavor.

Serves 4 to 6 as an appetizer

---

1 cup [240 g] cream cheese, at room temperature

½ cup [120 g] sour cream

One 12 oz [340 g] jar roasted artichoke hearts, drained, rinsed, and chopped into small pieces

1½ cups [120 g] shredded smoked Gouda

1 garlic clove, minced

1 tsp freshly squeezed lemon juice

⅛ tsp freshly ground black pepper

⅛ tsp salt

Preheat the oven to 350°F [180°C]. In a stand mixer fitted with the whisk attachment, beat the cream cheese and sour cream on medium speed until light and fluffy, about 30 seconds. Add the artichoke hearts, 1 cup [80 g] of the Gouda, the garlic, lemon juice, pepper, and salt and whisk on medium-high speed until completely combined, another 15 seconds.

Transfer the dip into an 8 in [20 cm] square baking dish or two 10 in [25 cm] oval baking dishes and top with the remaining ½ cup [40 g] of Gouda. Bake for 20 minutes or until bubbling around the edges. Turn on the broiler and broil for 3 minutes or until the top is browned.

Serve warm.

This dip can be made a day ahead of time (but wait to broil the top until right before serving) and stored in an airtight container in the refrigerator.

Caramelized Shallot Jam Dip

No party was complete at my house growing up without a bowl full of French onion dip (made using a Lipton dip packet and a tub of sour cream) and a bag of potato chips. Although I haven't abandoned this tradition completely, I've evolved it over the years to include versions of my own onion dip like this one.

Also, the shallot jam is delicious on its own with crackers and slices of sharp cheese.

Yields 2½ cups [325 g]

For the shallot jam

2 Tbsp unsalted butter

4 large shallots, thinly sliced

Fresh thyme leaves from 2 medium sprigs (½ packed tsp)

½ tsp salt, plus more for seasoning

¼ cup [60 ml] red wine vinegar

2 Tbsp brown sugar

1 Tbsp balsamic vinegar

For the dip

½ cup [120 g] sour cream

½ cup [120 g] Greek yogurt

1 Tbsp mayonnaise

¼ tsp garlic powder

Freshly ground black pepper

Salt

Olive oil, for drizzling

Thyme, for garnish

To make the shallot jam, in a medium skillet over medium-low heat, melt the butter. Add the shallots, thyme, and salt and sauté for 15 minutes, stirring often, until the shallots are very soft and starting to brown. Add the red wine vinegar, sugar, and balsamic vinegar and cook until almost all the liquid has evaporated and you are left with the consistency of thick jam, 5 to 8 more minutes. Remove from the heat and let cool. Taste and season with more salt, if needed.

To make the dip, in a medium bowl, mix together the cooled shallot jam, sour cream, Greek yogurt, mayonnaise, garlic powder, and pepper. Taste and adjust the seasoning, if needed, by adding more pepper or salt. Transfer the dip to a small serving bowl and and top it with the olive oil and thyme (see page 59) for my swirl technique).

This dip can be made 1 day ahead and stored in an airtight container in the refrigerator.

Homemade Ricotta with Warmed Tomatoes, Olives & Spicy Honey

It took a long time to finally convince myself to try making my own ricotta—it just seemed like it would be too much fuss. However, one day I was binge watching Ina Garten (as one does) and she made her own ricotta in less than half an hour. I was like, I gotta try this, and oh my—it turned out a hundred times more delicious than I even imagined (thank you, Ina!). Just make sure you don't purchase ultrapasteurized milk for this (mostly found with organic brands), as it won't curdle correctly. The mixture can boil over very quickly, so watch it closely and remove from the heat as soon as it starts to boil.

I call this my pizza dip because that's what it tastes like to me. It's basically all my favorite things to put on pizza (minus pineapple—didn't want to make this dip too controversial). Tomatoes are not in season in January in most parts of the United States, so I like to use cherry tomatoes since they can usually be found this time of year; warming them up brings out their juices and flavor. The spicy honey adds a finishing kick and a touch of sweetness—start with only drizzling half of the honey and tasting it, since some batches of tomatoes may be sweeter than others.

Yields about 3 cups [660 g]

For the ricotta

5 cups [1.2 L] whole milk

1½ cups [360 ml] heavy cream

1 tsp salt

3 Tbsp freshly squeezed lemon juice

For everything else

1 Tbsp olive oil

1 garlic clove, minced

1 tsp dried oregano

1½ cups [240 g] cherry tomatoes, halved

⅔ cups [110 g] kalamata olives, chopped

½ tsp salt

¼ cup [85 g] honey

2 tsp chili garlic sauce (I use Huy Fong Foods)

Freshly ground black pepper

Torn basil leaves, for garnish

To make the ricotta, pour the milk, heavy cream, and salt into a medium enamel or stainless steel pot and stir to combine. Bring to a boil over medium heat, stirring occasionally. Remove from the heat, stir in the lemon juice, and let sit for 1 minute to curdle.

Place a fine-mesh sieve over a large bowl and pour the ricotta mixture into the strainer. Let the mixture strain for 30 minutes, stirring every few minutes to help speed up the process, until the ricotta has reached your desired consistency. Discard the whey that has collected in the bowl.

Spread the ricotta in a small serving dish and set aside.

Meanwhile, in a small skillet over medium heat, warm the olive oil. Add the garlic and oregano and cook for 30 seconds or until the garlic darkens, turns brown, and becomes very fragrant. Add the tomatoes, olives, and salt and cook, stirring often,

until the tomatoes have softened but haven't lost their shape, about 5 minutes. Spoon the tomato-olive mixture over the fresh ricotta.

Wipe the skillet clean and add the honey and chili garlic sauce. Whisk continuously over medium heat until combined and the honey has become thin and runny, about 20 seconds. Drizzle half of the honey over the tomato-olive mixture. Taste and add more honey, if you'd like it sweeter and spicier. Season with pepper and garnish with basil leaves.

The ricotta can be made and stored in an airtight container in the refrigerator for 2 days before serving. Wait to make everything else until right before serving.

VALENTINE'S DAY CHOCOLATE FONDUE

Hot take: I hate going out to eat on Valentine's Day. Restaurants are crowded, you have to bug your significant other at least ten times to make the reservation, the menu is usually smaller to encourage faster table turnover, and it always feels like a bigger to-do than it is enjoyable. Instead, my favorite way to spend the evening is to make Wyatt cook for me (something that doesn't happen often) while I enjoy a glass of my favorite wine (anything with bubbles, please!) and snuggle with a blanket on the couch. Or better yet, we skip dinner altogether and Wyatt makes me a batch of chocolate fondue, then we spend the evening indulging in all the things we can find in the cabinets that are worth dipping in chocolate.

The fondue recipes ahead are very generous, so plan to have leftovers if it's just two of you. You could also consider serving this as dessert when having guests over.

Styling Notes

It's worth investing in a fondue pot for this spread, as it'll give you the option to keep the fondue warm while serving. I like to set the pot in the middle of a serving tray and create mounds of dipping options around it for an abundant vibe.

Make-Ahead Game Plan

The Brown Butter–Sour Cream Pound Cake (page 229) can be made the day before—wrap it in aluminum foil and store it at room temperature. The fondues are best made up to 1 hour before serving (keep them warm until ready to serve) and the spread can be assembled 30 minutes before serving.

Drink Pairing

Depending on whether you prefer red or white wine, choose a port wine or a sparkling white to go with this.

Wyatt's Sidebar

No meat necessary for this one!

Spread Type

Abundance Spread

Serves 2 to 4 generously

1 batch Dark Chocolate–Orange Fondue (page 226), Horchata-Spiced White Chocolate Fondue (page 227), or both, and plan for leftovers!

2 servings Brown Butter–Sour Cream Pound Cake (page 229)

3 to 4 cups [420 to 560 g] (depending on how hungry you are) dipping items (such as strawberries, pineapple pieces, banana slices, seedless grapes, figs, pretzels, potato chips, orange slices, vanilla wafers, graham crackers, marshmallows, etc.)

1 cup [roughly 30 g] garnish options (such as chopped peanuts, chopped pistachios, chopped pecans, fresh mint, fresh basil, crushed pretzels, flaky sea salt, etc.)

Transfer the warm fondue to a fondue pot (to keep warm) or a ceramic bowl and wait to put it out until right before enjoying. Place the fondue pot on a serving tray and any garnish options in individual bowls. Fill in the remaining space on the tray with the pound cake and dipping items.

Serve right away.

Flavor Combination Ideas	Dark Chocolate–Orange Fondue (page 226) + pineapple pieces + fresh mint	Horchata-Spiced White Chocolate Fondue (page 227) + Brown Butter–Sour Cream Pound Cake (page 229) + crushed pretzels	Dark Chocolate–Orange Fondue (page 226) + potato chips + flaky sea salt

Dark Chocolate—
Orange Fondue

Horchata-Spiced
White Chocolate Fondue

Brown Butter-
Sour Cream Pound
Cake

Dark Chocolate– Orange Fondue

Do you remember those balls of orange-flavored chocolate that came wrapped like they were oranges, and you could lightly smash them to break off the "orange segments"? Maybe they are still around (I'm not sure!) but we always got them in our Easter baskets when I was a kid. Anyhow, this fondue was inspired by that nostalgic flavor.

Serves 2

---

1 cup [240 ml] heavy cream

¼ cup [60 ml] juice from 1 medium orange

12 oz [340 g] 60% bittersweet chocolate, chopped into small chunks

⅛ tsp salt

Zest from 1 medium orange

In a small saucepan over medium heat, combine the heavy cream and orange juice. Let warm just until small bubbles start to appear around the edges, about 2 minutes. Remove from the heat and stir in the chocolate and salt. Once the chocolate has melted and a thick sauce has formed, whisk in the orange zest.

Return the saucepan to the stove and cook over low heat until warmed to the temperature of hot fudge.

Transfer the mixture to a fondue pot over a small flame, or keep warm on the stove over low heat. Serve right away.

Horchata-Spiced White Chocolate Fondue

Both a cinnamon stick and ground cinnamon are used in this recipe to give an extra punch of cinnamon flavor (the main flavor in this fondue besides the white chocolate, inspired by the refreshing Mexican rice milk). You'll be grinding the cinnamon stick in your high-speed blender along with the heavy cream, but don't fret if it doesn't break up completely since you'll then strain the mixture.

Serves 2

---

1 cup [240 ml] heavy cream

¼ cup [50 g] long-grain rice

1 cinnamon stick

1 Tbsp to ¼ cup [60 ml] whole milk (optional)

12 oz [340 g] white baking chocolate, chopped into small chunks

½ tsp vanilla extract

½ tsp ground cinnamon

⅛ tsp salt

Place the heavy cream, rice, and cinnamon stick in a blender and blend on high speed until the rice is chopped into small pieces, about 5 seconds. If too thick, add milk 1 Tbsp at a time to loosen the mixture. Transfer to the refrigerator and let chill for 2 hours.

Strain the cream mixture through a fine-mesh sieve into a small bowl—the cream will be thick, so use a spoon to push the mixture through the sieve. Transfer the cream to a small saucepan over medium heat and discard the solids from the sieve. Heat the cream until small bubbles start to appear around the edges. Remove from the heat and stir in the white chocolate, vanilla, ground cinnamon, and salt. Stir until the chocolate is melted and the mixture is smooth.

Return the saucepan to the stove and cook over low heat until warmed to the temperature of hot fudge.

Transfer the mixture to a fondue pot over a small flame or keep warm on the stove over low heat. Serve right away.

Brown Butter– Sour Cream Pound Cake

Browning the butter is an extra step, but the nutty aroma it gives to the final loaf is completely worth the effort. Also, there are two important notes to keep in mind to create a light and airy pound cake: Let the butter solidify again after you brown it, and really beat each egg into the batter after adding it to create air pockets in the batter.

Serves 6 to 8 generously

½ cup [110 g] unsalted butter, cut into large pieces

1 cup [200 g] brown sugar

½ cup [100 g] granulated sugar

3 eggs, at room temperature

1½ cups [210 g] all-purpose flour

¼ tsp baking soda

¼ tsp salt

½ cup [120 g] sour cream

1 tsp vanilla extract

In a medium skillet over medium heat, melt the butter, whisking frequently. Once melted, continue to cook, letting the butter foam and form brown specks at the bottom of the skillet (it will also begin to smell nutty), about 5 minutes. Remove from the heat and transfer to a heatproof glass bowl. Transfer to the freezer and let cool for 20 to 25 minutes or until solidified.

Preheat the oven to 325°F [165°C] and grease a standard 8 in [20 cm] loaf pan.

In the bowl of a stand mixer fitted with the paddle attachment, cream together the butter, brown sugar, and granulated sugar on high speed until light and fluffy, 3 to 5 minutes. Add the eggs, 1 at a time, beating for a full 30 seconds on high speed between each addition until completely incorporated. After the third egg, the batter should be at least double in size and light in color.

Meanwhile, whisk together the flour, baking soda, and salt in a small mixing bowl.

With the stand mixer running on low speed, add one-third of the flour mixture, then one-third of the sour cream, then repeat with the remaining flour mixture and sour cream. Add the vanilla and beat on low speed until completely combined.

Pour the batter into the prepared loaf pan and bake for 1 hour or until a toothpick inserted into the center comes out clean. Remove from the oven and transfer to a wire rack to cool before cutting.

Wrap the cake in aluminum foil and store leftovers at room temperature for up to 3 days.

MOTHER'S DAY SPRING MINESTRONE SOUP SPREAD

Whether this is an intimate celebration of your mom with just your immediate family or a big gathering to celebrate many women in your life, this soup spread is an effortless way to show them you care.

Make-Ahead Game Plan

The Spring Mine-strone (page **234**) can be made up to 3 days ahead of time (wait to add the pasta until you are warming it up for serving so it doesn't get overcooked) and stored in an airtight container in the refrig-erator—warm it up on the stove when ready to serve. The Lemon-Pea Gremolata (page **237**) can be made the day before and stored in an airtight container in the refrigerator—make sure to bring it to room tem-perature before serving. You can start prepping all the toppings an hour before guests arrive, and assembling the spread 30 minutes before.

Drink Pairing

Whip up a batch of white sangria to serve in a pitcher alongside this spread: Combine one 750 ml bottle chilled dry white wine, 2 cups [240 g] sliced fruit (think straw-berries, lemons, limes, peaches, etc.), ¼ cup [60 ml] fruit liquor (such as Grand Marnier or Cointreau), ¼ cup [3 g] fresh mint leaves, and 1 cup [240 ml] sparkling water.

Styling Notes

Pick out an array of small, mismatched ceramic dishes to use for all the garnish options.

Spread Type

Family Style

Wyatt's Sidebar

Set out a plate of thin strips of prosciutto for guests to top their soup with.

Serves 8

1 batch **Spring Minestrone** (page 234)

1 batch **Lemon-Pea Gremolata**
  (page 237)

1 cup shredded Parmesan cheese

½ cup [120 g] pesto

¼ cup [10 g] chopped dill

¼ cup [10 g] chopped chives

¼ cup [10 g] chopped fresh basil

¼ cup [5 g] arugula

2 Tbsp fresh thyme

8 lemon wedges (from 1 large lemon)

**8 slices toasted bread (from 1 baguette
  or ½ fresh loaf)**

Salt and freshly ground black pepper

Transfer the minestrone to a large serving pot and place it on the grazing table. Transfer all the the topping ingredients (except the bread, salt, and pepper) into individual serving bowls and arrange them around the minestrone pot. Add a plate of bread and small bowls of salt and pepper to the far right of the table so people can season at the end and grab a slice of bread for dunking.

Spring Minestrone

Season the soup both throughout the cooking process and also at the very end to make sure you end up with a robust flavor. I prefer to use low-sodium broth so I can have more control over the salt content, but feel free to start by adding less salt if you didn't purchase low-sodium broth.

Serves 8

---

2 Tbsp olive oil

2 celery stalks, diced

2 medium carrots, chopped

1 bunch asparagus, trimmed and cut into 1 in [2.5 cm] pieces

1 yellow onion, diced

2 garlic cloves, minced

1 Tbsp dried oregano

1½ tsp salt

1 tsp dried basil

1 tsp fresh thyme

2 Tbsp tomato paste

4 cups [960 ml] low-sodium vegetable broth

One 15 oz [430 g] can white beans (such as cannellini), rinsed

One 15 oz [430 g] can kidney beans, rinsed

One 14 oz [400 g] can fire-roasted diced tomatoes

1 cup [125 g] frozen green beans

1 cup [55 g] tubettini, orecchiette, or farfalle pasta

Freshly ground black pepper

Grated Parmesan cheese, for serving

Heat the olive oil in a large stockpot over medium heat. Add the celery, carrots, asparagus, and onion and sauté for 5 to 7 minutes or until vegetables are starting to soften and become fragrant. Add the garlic, oregano, ½ tsp of the salt, the basil, and thyme and sauté for another 30 seconds. Add the tomato paste, vegetable broth, white beans, kidney beans, fire-roasted tomatoes, green beans, and 1 cup [240 ml] of water. Turn the heat up to high to bring the mixture to a boil, then lower the heat to medium-low and simmer for 15 minutes to let the flavors meld.

Add the pasta and cook, covered, for an additional 5 to 10 minutes (check the directions on the package of pasta).

Remove from the heat and season with the remaining 1 tsp of salt and a few turns of pepper. Taste and adjust the seasonings as necessary. Garnish with Parmesan and serve right away.

Leftovers can be stored in an airtight container in the refrigerator for up to 3 days.

Lemon–Pea Gremolata

Lemon-Pea Gremolata

Instead of just garnishing your soup with fresh herbs, finish each bowl with this Lemon-Pea Gremolata to add brightness. You can also use it as a topping for pastas and salads.

Yields about 1 cup [135 g]

---

1 cup [120 g] frozen peas

Zest of 1 lemon

2 garlic cloves, finely grated (you can use the same zester you used for the lemon)

1 Tbsp chopped parsley

Bring a small saucepan of water to boil over high heat. Meanwhile, make an ice bath by placing 1 cup [140 g] of ice in a medium bowl and filling the bowl with enough water to cover the ice. Once the saucepan is boiling, add the peas and cook for 2 minutes. Drain and transfer the peas to the ice bath. Let cool for 5 minutes.

Drain and lightly chop the peas (some can be left whole). Toss them with the lemon zest, garlic, and chopped parsley.

SCHOOL'S OUT SUMMER LIMEADE PARTY

I wanted to include at least one drink spread that wasn't alcoholic, so I figured a limeade party would be a refreshing option for the summer months. Make sure to prepare the limeade in advance since it needs to chill for 2 hours.

Make-Ahead Game Plan

The Homemade Maraschino Cherries (page 245) can be made up to 1 week ahead and stored in an airtight container in the refrigerator. The lime juice can be squeezed the day before and stored in an airtight container in the refrigerator. The limeades can be mixed the morning of (minus the ice), and the fruit can be sliced at that time and all stored in airtight containers in the refrigerator. Assemble the spread 30 minutes before guests arrive but hold off on putting out the ice until right before they walk in the door.

Spread Type

Drink Station

Styling Notes

You'll want to whip up a few batches of limeade to serve in pitchers and then make a little platter display with the garnish options. I like to fan out the fruit so that each piece is overlapping the next piece slightly to keep it looking organized but full. Also, if it's citrus season, try to snag a few different varieties of oranges (such as blood oranges, Cara Cara, navel, etc.) to give extra color to the display.

Flavor Combination Ideas

Easy Limeade (page 240) + lime slices + fresh mint

Blackberry-Hibiscus Limeade (page 244) + muddled blackberries + orange slices + thyme

Easy Limeade (page 240) + Homemade Maraschino Cherries, with a few tablespoons of the juice (page 245) + lemon slices + fresh mint

Serves 12

1 batch Easy Limeade (page 240)

1 batch Blackberry-Hibiscus Limeade (page 244)

1 batch Homemade Maraschino Cherries (page 245)

6 cups [840 g] ice

1 cup [120 g] fresh strawberries, sliced

1 cup [120 g] fresh blackberries

3 limes, sliced

3 oranges, sliced

1 lemon, sliced

¼ cup [3 g] fresh mint

6 sprigs fresh thyme

Pour the two limeade batches into their own pitchers and place them next to a large serving platter. Place the Homemade Maraschino Cherries, ice, strawberries, and blackberries in their own serving bowls and set them on a large serving platter. Fill in the platter by fanning out the lime slices, orange slices, and lemon slices around the bowls. Fill in any empty space with the mint and thyme. Serve right away.

Easy Limeade

Juicing the limes will be a bit tedious, but the fresh juice you'll get from doing it yourself will be well worth the extra effort.

Makes 6 drinks

---

1 cup [200 g] sugar

6 cups [1.4 L] water, or 5 cups [1.2 L] water and 1 cup [240 ml] sparkling water

1 cup [240 ml] freshly squeezed lime juice (from about 12 medium or 16 small limes)

1 lime, sliced

In a small saucepan over medium-high heat, whisk together the sugar and 1 cup [240 ml] of the water. Bring to a simmer and whisk until the sugar is dissolved. Remove from the heat and set aside to cool.

Once cooled, combine the simple syrup with the lime juice and the remaining 5 cups [1.2 L] of water (or 4 cups [960 ml], if using sparkling water). Cover and let chill in the refrigerator for at least 2 hours.

When ready to serve, add 2 cups [280 g] of ice, the lime slices, and sparkling water, if using. Stir and serve.

The simple syrup can be made up to 1 week ahead and stored in an airtight container in the refrigerator.

Homemade Maraschino Cherries

Blackberry–Hibiscus Limeade

Look for food-grade dried hibiscus in either the tea section or herbs section of your local grocery store.

Makes 6 drinks

---

1 cup [200 g] sugar

6 cups [1.4 L] water, or 5 cups [1.2 L] water and 1 cup [240 ml] sparkling water

1 cup [120 g] blackberries

¼ cup [10 g] dried hibiscus leaves

1 in [2.5 cm] piece fresh ginger, peeled and grated

1 cup [240 ml] freshly squeezed lime juice (from about 12 medium or 16 small limes)

1 lime, sliced

In a small saucepan over medium-high heat, whisk together the sugar, 1 cup [240 ml] of the water, the blackberries, hibiscus leaves, and ginger. Bring to a simmer and whisk until the sugar is dissolved. Let simmer for 1 minute, cover, and remove from the heat. Let cool completely and then strain. Discard the solids.

Once cooled, combine the strained simple syrup with the lime juice and remaining 5 cups [1.2 L] of water (or 4 cups [960 ml], if using sparkling water). Cover and let chill in the refrigerator for at least 2 hours.

When ready to serve, add 2 cups [280 g] of ice, the lime slices, and sparkling water, if using. Stir and serve.

The simple syrup can be made up to 1 week ahead and stored in an airtight container in the refrigerator.

Homemade Maraschino Cherries

Although not as neon red (maybe that's a good thing?) as the iconic maraschino cherries we are used to seeing at chain restaurants, these homemade marachino cherries are a super easy and delicious garnish for all your cocktail needs.

Yields about 2 cups [500 g]

½ cup [100 g] sugar

¼ cup [60 ml] orange juice (from 1 medium orange)

Seeds from ½ vanilla bean, pod discarded

1 cinnamon stick

1¼ cups [180 g] pitted and destemmed sweet cherries (fresh or frozen)

In a medium saucepan over high heat, combine 1 cup [240 ml] of water, the sugar, orange juice, vanilla seeds, and cinnamon stick and bring to a boil. Add the cherries and let the mixture come back up to a simmer. Lower the heat to low and let simmer for 5 minutes or until the cherries start to soften.

Remove from the heat, cover, and let cool completely.

Use right away or transfer to an airtight jar (with the liquid) and store in the refrigerator for up to 1 week.

FALL GRAZING BOARD

OK, so maybe fall isn't an official holiday, but it's my favorite time to host a get-together because the bugs have finally disappeared and the cooler air is perfect for casual gatherings. Know someone celebrating a birthday in the fall? Invite them over and make this board for them! Looking for an excuse to host a bonfire? Call up some friends and share this board with the group! Just want to visit with your some of your favorite people before the craziness of the holiday begins? Invite them over and let them indulge in this board!

Styling Notes

Keep this board simple to let the ingredients really shine. Place the serving bowl with the hummus on the board first and arrange the additional toppings around it. I love to use a dark surface here to bring a moody feel to the board, which is an ideal contrast to the summer food you've been munching on for the past several months.

Wyatt's Sidebar

Choose a salami like soppressata, pepperoni, or smoked lardo to complement the other components of the board.

Make-Ahead Game Plan

The Butternut Squash Brown Butter Pecan Hummus (page 249) can be made the day before (minus the brown butter topping) and stored in an airtight container in the refrigerator. Bring out all the cheese an hour before serving, and the cured meat 30 minutes before serving, so it can all come to room temperature. Feel free to assemble the spread up to 30 minutes before guests arrive.

Drink Pairing

Enjoy with a warming whiskey sour! To make one, add 2 oz [60 ml] of bourbon, ¾ oz [20 ml] of freshly squeezed lemon juice, and ½ oz [15 ml] of simple syrup to a shaker with ice and shake. Strain into a cocktail glass and serve with an orange peel or Homemade Maraschino Cherry (page 245).

Spread Type

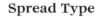

Statement Piece

Serves 6

1 batch Butternut Squash Brown
   Butter Pecan Hummus (page 249)

6 oz [170 g] blue cheese

6 oz [170 g] salty hard cheese (such as
   Manchego or Asiago)

¾ cup [225 g] apple butter or fig jam

6 Tbsp [90 g] stone-ground mustard

3 Tbsp honey

1 cup [160 g] grapes

¾ cup [105 g] salted nuts (such as
   almonds or walnuts)

¾ cup [120 g] mixed marinated olives

1 sliced apple or pear tossed with 1 tsp
   freshly squeezed lemon juice

12 slices baguette

6 oz [170 g] crackers

Fresh tarragon or rosemary,
   for garnish

Strategically place the Butternut Squash Brown Butter Pecan Hummus, blue cheese, and salty hard cheese in different areas of the serving board. Place the apple butter, mustard, and honey into individual small bowls and add them to the serving board. Fill in the remaining space with the grapes, nuts, olives, apple, baguette, and crackers. Add a few sprigs of tarragon or rosemary to the board to fill in any lingering open spots.

Butternut Squash Brown Butter Pecan Hummus

Butternut Squash Brown Butter Pecan Hummus

If you find yourself with some extra time, feel free to peel the chickpeas beforehand for an extra-creamy hummus.

Serves 6

½ cup [110 g] tahini

⅓ cup [80 ml] olive oil

2 Tbsp freshly squeezed lemon juice

2 garlic cloves, peeled and grated

½ tsp cinnamon

½ tsp salt

Two 15 oz [430 g] cans chickpeas, drained and rinsed

One 15 oz [430 g] can puréed butternut squash

4 Tbsp [55 g] unsalted butter

¼ cup [30 g] chopped pecans

Freshly ground black pepper

Add the tahini, olive oil, lemon juice, garlic, cinnamon, and salt to a food processor fitted with the blade attachment and process until completely combined, about 30 seconds. Add the chickpeas and butternut squash and let the food processor run for 2 minutes or until the hummus has expanded and is smooth and light.

In a small saucepan over medium heat, melt the butter. Continue to cook, watching it closely and swirling the butter around the pan every few seconds, until it bubbles and specks of brown butter start to form, 3 to 4 minutes. Add the pecans and toss to coat. Remove from the heat.

Transfer the hummus to a shallow serving bowl and and top it with the pecans and brown butter (see page 59 for my swirl technique). Sprinkle with pepper and serve right away with crackers.

THANKSGIVING DESSERT TABLE

Is Thanksgiving even Thanksgiving without pies? I love being in charge of cooking for Thanksgiving but I find that I get bored easily with making the same recipes every year, so I'm always looking for new twists on the old classics. This is exactly why all the recipes in this spread check the boxes for the three pies I'm required to make every year (pumpkin, apple, and pecan) but include fun flavor variations.

Make-Ahead Game Plan

The pie dough and shortbread crust can be made up to 3 days ahead and stored in the refrigerator. Pies can be baked the day before serving. To store, wrap them all in plastic wrap and store the Apple, Black Sesame & Cardamom Crumble Pie (page 259) and Salted Pecan Tart with Caraway-Rye Shortbread Crust (page 254) at room temperature, and the Buttermilk-Maple Pumpkin Pie (page 256) in the fridge.

Drink Pairing

I love to savor a strong cup of black coffee with my sweets. Alternatively, you could serve this with unsweetened iced tea for those who are looking for something more refreshing.

Styling Notes

Since the pies and tart are the stars for this spread, we keep the additional topping options very minimal. With that in mind, focus on creating a beautiful tablescape with a lovely tablecloth, seasonal flowers, and nice dinnerware.

Spread Type

Assembly Spread

Wyatt's Sidebar

No need to add meat to this one!

Flavor Combination Ideas

Salted Pecan Tart with Caraway-Rye Shortbread Crust (page 254) + vanilla ice cream + toasted sesame seeds

Apple, Black Sesame & Cardamom Crumble Pie (page 259) + Tahini Caramel Sauce (page 261)

Buttermilk-Maple Pumpkin Pie (page 256) + whipped cream

Serves 15

1 Salted Pecan Tart with Caraway-Rye Shortbread Crust (page 254)

1 Buttermilk-Maple Pumpkin Pie (page 256)

1 Apple, Black Sesame & Cardamom Crumble Pie (page 259)

1 batch Tahini Caramel Sauce (page 261)

3 pints [800 g] vanilla bean ice cream

4 cups [240 g] whipped cream

¼ cup [35 g] chopped peanuts

2 Tbsp toasted sesame seeds

1 Tbsp flaky sea salt

Place the tart and pies on your dessert table and add pie servers to each one. Place the caramel sauce, ice cream, whipped cream, peanuts, sesame seeds, and sea salt into individual bowls and set them near the pies as topping options.

Apple, Black Sesame & Cardamom Crumble

Salted Pecan Tart with Caraway-Rye Shortbread Crust

The savory rye and caraway really work to tame the sweetness of the filling so you end up with deliciously sweet and savory tart.

Yields one 9 in [23 cm] tart

For the crust

2½ tsp caraway seeds

½ cup [60 g] sifted all-purpose flour

½ cup [55 g] dark rye flour

⅓ cup [40 g] confectioners' sugar

¼ tsp salt

½ cup [110 g] cold unsalted butter, cut into small pieces

For the filling

1 cup [120 g] roughly chopped pecans

¾ cup [150 g] brown sugar

¼ cup [55 g] unsalted butter

½ cup [120 ml] maple syrup

2 eggs, lightly beaten

1 tsp vanilla extract

½ tsp salt

To make the crust, lightly grease a 9 in [23 cm] tart pan. In a small skillet over medium heat, toast the seeds for 2 to 3 minutes or until brown and fragrant.

Transfer the seeds to a food processor fitted with the blade attachment and add the all-purpose flour. Pulse a few times to break down the seeds. Add the rye flour, confectioners' sugar, and salt. Pulse a few times to combine and then add the butter. Pulse for 30 seconds or until a ball of dough forms. Press the dough evenly into the bottom and up the sides of the tart pan, patching any holes. Pierce all over with a fork, making sure not to poke all the way through.

Preheat the oven to 400°F [200°C] and transfer the tart pan to the freezer for 15 minutes. Once chilled, bake for 15 minutes or until browned. Remove from the oven and transfer to a wire rack to cool completely.

To make the filling, lower the oven temperature to 325°F [165°C]. Spread the pecans in a single layer in the crust. In a medium saucepan over medium heat, melt the brown sugar and butter, whisking often, 1 to 3 minutes. Remove from the heat and cool slightly, then whisk in the maple syrup, eggs, vanilla, and salt. Pour the mixture over the pecans and stir to submerge the pecans.

Bake for 35 to 40 minutes or until the center has set. Remove from the oven and transfer to a wire rack. Let cool completely before slicing. Store leftovers wrapped in plastic wrap in the refrigerator for up to 2 days.

Buttermilk–Maple Pumpkin Pie

I love to pile a thick layer of homemade whipped cream onto this pie when serving.

Yields one 9 in [23 cm] pie

For the crust

1¼ cup [150 g] sifted all-purpose flour

½ tsp salt

½ tsp granulated sugar

½ cup [110 g] cold unsalted European-style butter, cut into small pieces or shredded with a large box grater

¼ cup [60 ml] ice-cold water

For the filling

One 15 oz [430 g] can pumpkin purée

1 cup [240 ml] buttermilk

¼ cup [60 g] maple syrup

2 eggs, lightly beaten

½ cup [100 g] brown sugar

½ tsp cinnamon

¼ tsp allspice

¼ tsp ground ginger

⅛ tsp salt

Whipped cream, for topping (optional)

continued

To make the crust, in a large mixing bowl, whisk together the flour, salt, and granulated sugar. Add the butter and, using a pastry blender or clean hands, work the butter into the flour mixture until all the butter pieces are pea-size or smaller. Drizzle in the water and use a spatula, wooden spoon, or clean hands to mix until a dough ball has formed.

Shape the dough into a disc 2 in [5 cm] thick, scraping up any lingering pieces from the bowl, and wrap it in plastic wrap. Transfer the disc to the refrigerator to chill for at least 2 hours.

Once chilled, lightly flour a work surface and roll out the pie dough into an 11 in [28 cm] circle. Transfer the dough to a 9 in [23 cm] pie pan, letting the excess hang over the edges. Roll the excess dough up to where you want your pie crust to end and crimp the dough. Transfer to the freezer and let chill for at least 15 minutes before baking.

Preheat the oven to 450°F [230°C]. When ready to bake, remove the pie crust from the freezer and tightly cover it with a sheet of aluminum foil. Add enough pie weights or dried beans to completely fill up to the rim of the crust. Bake for 15 minutes or until the edges are just starting to turn golden. Remove the foil and weights and bake for another 10 to 12 minutes or until the crust is starting to get golden

all over. Transfer to a wire rack and let cool completely.

Lower the oven to 325°F [165°C].

To make the filling, in a medium mixing bowl, whisk together the pumpkin purée, buttermilk, maple syrup, and eggs. In another medium mixing bowl, whisk together the brown sugar, cinnamon, allspice, ginger, and salt. Whisk the dry ingredients into the wet ingredients until combined.

Pour the filling into the prepared pie crust and bake for 40 to 50 minutes or until the filling no longer jiggles and the crust is browned. Let cool completely before serving with whipped cream, if desired.

Store leftovers tightly wrapped in plastic wrap in the refrigerator for up to 2 days.

Apple, Black Sesame & Cardamom Crumble Pie

This might be one of my favorite recipes in this whole book. I took the apple pie, a dish thought of as a symbol of America, and added in Indian accent ingredients that don't overwhelm the apples but instead add a strikingly delicious new flavor profile to the pie. The whole thing is just so darn delicious . . . what more is there to say?

Yields one 9 in [23 cm] pie

For the crust

1¼ cup [150 g] sifted all-purpose flour

½ tsp salt

½ tsp granulated sugar

½ cup [110 g] cold unsalted European-style butter, cut into small pieces or shredded with a large box grater

¼ cup [60 ml] ice-cold water

For the topping

1 cup [120 g] sifted all-purpose flour

¼ cup [50 g] brown sugar

1½ Tbsp black sesame seeds

¾ tsp ground cardamom

¼ tsp salt

6 Tbsp [85 g] unsalted butter, cut into cubes

1 Tbsp tahini

2 Tbsp whole milk

For the filling

3 lb [1.4 kg] mixed apples (such as Golden Delicious, Granny Smith, and Gala), peeled and sliced ¼ in [6 mm] thick

4 Tbsp [55 g] unsalted butter, melted

1 Tbsp freshly squeezed lemon juice

½ cup [100 g] granulated sugar

½ cup [100 g] packed light brown sugar

2 Tbsp all-purpose flour

2 Tbsp cornstarch

1 tsp ground cinnamon

½ tsp cardamom

⅛ tsp salt

1 egg, lightly beaten and mixed with 1 Tbsp water

continued

To make the crust, in a large mixing bowl, whisk together the flour, salt, and granulated sugar. Add the butter and, using a pastry blender or clean hands, work the butter into the flour mixture until all the butter pieces are pea-size or smaller. Drizzle in the water and use a spatula, wooden spoon, or clean hands to mix until a dough ball has formed.

Shape the dough into a disc 2 in [5 cm] thick, scraping up any lingering pieces from the bowl, and wrap it in plastic wrap. Transfer the disc to the refrigerator to chill for at least 2 hours.

Once chilled, lightly flour a work surface and roll out the pie dough into an 11 in [28 cm] circle. Transfer the dough to a 9 in [23 cm] pie pan, letting the excess hang over the edges. Roll the excess dough up to where you want your pie crust to end and crimp the dough. Transfer to the freezer and let chill for at least 15 minutes.

To make the topping, preheat the oven to 375°F [190°C]. In a medium mixing bowl, whisk together the flour, brown sugar, sesame seeds, cardamom, and salt until combined. Add the butter and, using clean hands or a pastry blender, work the butter into the dough until all the butter pieces are pea-size or smaller. Drizzle in the tahini

and mix until combined (you'll begin to see large crumb pieces coming together, which is exactly what you want). Add the milk and mix until the dough has turned into large crumbs. Cover and place the bowl in the refrigerator to keep the topping mixture cold while you prepare the filling.

To make the filling, in a large mixing bowl, toss together the apple slices, butter, and lemon juice. In a medium mixing bowl, whisk together the granulated sugar, brown sugar, flour, cornstarch, cinnamon, cardamom, and salt until combined. Add the flour mixture to the apple mixture and toss to coat all the apples.

Remove the pie crust from the freezer and transfer the apple filling into the pie crust, spreading it in an even layer. Sprinkle the crumb topping over the apples. Brush the edges of the pie crust with the egg wash.

Loosely cover the pie with aluminum foil and bake for 20 minutes. Remove the foil and bake for an additional 40 to 50 minutes or until the crumb on top is browned. Remove the pie from the oven and transfer it to a wire rack. Let cool completely before serving.

Store leftovers wrapped in plastic wrap at room temperature for up to 2 days.

Tahini Caramel Sauce

This is one of the trickier recipes in the book, so you'll want to follow the directions very carefully. As it's very easy to overcook the caramel sauce, I highly recommend using a candy thermometer, or you might end up with rock-hard caramel. Also, make sure not to stir the mixture while it's boiling or else you could end up splashing the mixture onto the sides of the pan, which could result in grainy caramel. And finally, be very careful when pouring the cream into the boiling sugar because it will bubble and the mixture is very hot! When done correctly, the end result is a decadent but thin caramel sauce perfect for drizzling over your pies or ice cream.

Yields about 1²/₃ cup [400 ml]

---

1 cup [200 g] granulated sugar

1 cup [240 ml] heavy cream

2 Tbsp unsalted butter

½ tsp kosher salt

¼ cup [55 g] tahini

In a medium saucepan over medium heat, whisk together the sugar and ¼ cup [60 ml] of cold water until a thick paste has formed. Cook, without stirring, for 8 to 10 minutes or until your mixture reaches about 350°F [180°C] on your candy thermometer (the sugar should be just starting to turn amber at this point).

Meanwhile, in a small saucepan over low heat, warm the heavy cream. When the sugar mixture is ready, slowly whisk in the warm cream until fully incorporated and the mixture has stopped bubbling. Remove from the heat and stir in the butter and salt. Finally, stir in the tahini. Serve warm.

Leftover sauce can be stored in an airtight container in the refrigerator for up to 1 week.

CHRISTMAS MORNING DUTCH BABY PARTY

A lazy holiday morning is only made better with a big breakfast spread that serves your entire family. It's best to make one Dutch baby at a time and whip up the next batch of batter while one bakes. Serve as soon as they emerge from the oven, puffy and golden. You can transfer each finished Dutch baby onto a baking sheet and either set them on top of the oven to keep warm, or, if you'd like to sit down with your guests, pop them back into the warm oven right before serving to warm them back up, and then serve all three at once.

Make-Ahead Game Plan

The creamy topping options can be made the day before and stored in airtight containers in the refrigerator. The fruit can be sliced the night before and stored in airtight containers in the refrigerator (just spritz it with water when serving if it looks dry). Feel free to assemble the toppings into serving bowls while the Dutch babies bake, and wait to fry the eggs, if using, until right before serving.

Styling Notes

Because there is so much going on with this spread, plan to arrange your table with all the fixings before baking the Dutch babies. Create a varied look on the table by using a mixture of small and large shallow bowls. If possible, color-coordinate your tableware, using items from the same table set or color palette (I love using neutral ceramic bowls for this).

Spread Type

Buffet Style or Family Style

Drink Pairing

Make the Boozy Bloody Mary Bar (page 192) and also whip up a batch of strong coffee to linger over while you are making and eating this spread. If coffee and boozy morning drinks aren't your thing, you could also put out a pot of hot water and a selection of tea options (my favorite morning tea is a rooibos chai, but other more Christmassy teas, such as a cinnamon-vanilla blend, feel special and are fun to try too).

Wyatt's Sidebar

Cooked, thinly sliced smoked deli ham is a perfect pairing with the Cheddar-Thyme Dutch Baby (page 269) and a fried egg.

Serves 10 to 12

1 Standard Dutch Baby (page 266)

1 Cheddar-Thyme Dutch Baby (page 269)

1 Grapefruit-Ricotta Dutch Baby (page 267)

1 batch Chocolate-Chai Mascarpone (page 270)

1 batch Vanilla Bean & Honey Chèvre (page 273)

1 batch Savory Ranch Crème Fraîche (page 274)

1 cup [240 ml] maple syrup

1 cup [240 g] ricotta (store-bought or homemade from recipe on page 220)

½ cup [110 g] butter, at room temperature

¼ cup [85 g] honey

2 cups [approximately 280 g] fresh fruit (such as strawberries, blueberries, raspberries, orange slices, banana slices, etc.)

¼ cup [5 g] fresh herbs (such as thyme, mint, and parsley) or green onions

Additional optional items: scrambled or fried eggs, avocado slices, tomato slices

Transfer the Dutch babies to serving trays or keep them in their baking pans and cut them into quarters. Place all the sauces and toppings into their own individual bowls and arrange them on the serving table. Add spoons to the sauces and ricotta. Add a butter knife to the butter and any additional serving utensils that will be needed to the board. Serve right away.

Flavor Combination Ideas	Standard Dutch Baby (page 266) + Chocolate-Chai Mascarpone (page 270) + maple syrup + banana slices	Cheddar-Thyme Dutch Baby (page 269) + Savory Ranch Crème Fraîche (page 274) + fried egg + fresh thyme	Grapefruit-Ricotta Dutch Baby (page 267) + Vanilla Bean & Honey Chèvre (page 273) + blueberries and raspberries + honey

Standard Dutch Baby

This basic recipe is the perfect blank canvas for guests to load with whatever toppings they are craving (sweet or savory!).

Yields one 12 in [30.5 cm] Dutch baby

4 Tbsp [55 g] butter

¾ cup [180 ml] whole milk, at room temperature

¾ cup [105 g] all-purpose flour

3 large eggs, at room temperature

2 Tbsp sugar

¼ tsp kosher salt

Place a heavy 12 in [30 cm] skillet in the oven and preheat the oven to 425°F [220°C].

In a small microwave-safe bowl, microwave 2 Tbsp of the butter for 30 seconds or until melted. If a few solid pieces remain, swirl the butter around to melt them. Set aside and let cool to room temperature.

In a high-speed blender, blend the milk, flour, eggs, sugar, salt, and the melted butter until completely smooth, about 20 seconds, scraping down the sides of the blender with a spatula as needed.

Carefully remove the hot skillet from the oven and add the remaining 2 Tbsp of butter. Swirl the butter around until melted and the entire bottom of the skillet is coated. Pour the batter into the skillet and return it to the oven. Bake for 20 to 22 minutes or until the sides have browned and the top is puffed.

Remove the skillet from the oven and transfer it to a cutting board. Cut the Dutch baby into four triangles (like you cut would a pie) and serve right away.

Grapefruit–Ricotta Dutch Baby

This is a rich, sophisticated approach to a Dutch baby. The grapefruit adds a floral, citrussy flavor.

Yields one 12 in [30.5 cm] Dutch baby

4 Tbsp [55 g] butter

¾ cup [180 ml] whole milk, at room temperature

¾ cup [105 g] all-purpose flour

¾ cup [180 g] ricotta

3 large eggs, at room temperature

2 Tbsp plus 1 tsp sugar

2 tsp grapefruit zest

½ tsp vanilla extract

¼ tsp kosher salt

1 Tbsp grapefruit juice

Place a heavy 12 in [30 cm] skillet in the oven and preheat the oven to 425°F [220°C].

In a small microwave-safe bowl, microwave 2 Tbsp of the butter for 30 seconds or until melted. If a few solid pieces remain, swirl the butter around to melt them. Set aside and let cool to room temperature.

In a high-speed blender, blend together the milk, flour, ¼ cup [60 g] of the ricotta, the eggs, 2 Tbsp of the sugar, 1 tsp of the grapefruit zest, the vanilla, salt, and the melted butter until completely smooth, about 20 seconds, scraping down the sides of the blender with a spatula as needed.

Carefully remove the hot skillet from the oven and add the remaining 2 Tbsp of butter. Swirl the butter around until melted and the entire bottom of the skillet is coated. Pour the batter into skillet and return it to the oven. Bake for 20 to 22 minutes or until the sides have browned and the top is puffed.

Meanwhile, combine the remaining ½ cup [120 g] of ricotta, the grapefruit juice, the remaining 1 tsp of sugar, and the remaining 1 tsp of grapefruit zest in a small bowl. Set aside.

Remove the skillet from the oven and transfer it to a cutting board. Cut the Dutch baby into four triangles (like you cut would a pie) and serve right away with the ricotta mixture.

Cheddar-Thyme Dutch Baby

I love how subtle the thyme is in this savory version, but it would also be delicious with finely chopped fresh sage or rosemary.

Yields one 12 in [30.5 cm] Dutch baby

---

4 Tbsp [55 g] butter

¾ cup [180 ml] whole milk, at room temperature

¾ cup [105 g] all-purpose flour

3 large eggs, at room temperature

2 Tbsp sugar

1 tsp fresh thyme leaves

¼ tsp kosher salt

1 cup [80 g] shredded aged Cheddar cheese

Place a heavy 12 in [30 cm] skillet in the oven and preheat the oven to 425°F [220°C].

In a small microwave-safe bowl, microwave 2 Tbsp of the butter for 30 seconds or until melted. If a few solid pieces remain, swirl the butter around to melt them. Set aside and let cool to room temperature.

In a high speed blender, blend together the milk, flour, eggs, sugar, thyme, salt, and the melted butter until completely smooth, about 20 seconds, scraping down the sides of the blender with a spatula as needed.

Carefully remove the hot skillet from the oven and add the remaining 2 Tbsp of butter. Swirl the butter around until melted and the entire bottom of the skillet is coated. Pour the batter into the skillet and return it to the oven. Bake for 15 minutes, sprinkle the Cheddar over the top of the Dutch baby, and bake for an additional 5 to 7 minutes or until the cheese has melted on top.

Remove the skillet from the oven and transfer it to a cutting board. Cut the Dutch baby into four triangles (like you would cut a pie) and serve right away.

Chocolate-Chai Mascarpone

Who needs whipped cream when you can dollop this rich and creamy mascarpone on top?

In a medium bowl, whisk together all the ingredients until a smooth spread forms. Serve right away.

Yields approximately ¾ cup [170 g]

½ cup [120 g] mascarpone cheese

3 Tbsp whole milk

1½ Tbsp honey

1 Tbsp cocoa powder

½ tsp cinnamon

¼ tsp nutmeg

¼ tsp ground ginger

⅛ tsp ground cloves

⅛ tsp salt

Vanilla Bean
& Honey
Chèvre

If you don't have any vanilla bean pods on hand, you can substitute with 1 tsp vanilla extract.

In a medium bowl, whisk together all the ingredients until a smooth spread forms. Serve right away.

Yields approximately ¾ cup [180 g]

½ cup [120 g] chèvre, at room temperature

2 oz [55 g] cream cheese, at room temperature

1 Tbsp honey

1 Tbsp whole milk

Seeds from ½ vanilla bean, pod discarded

Savory Ranch Crème Fraîche

Homemade ranch gets an indulgent upgrade with the addition of crème fraîche!

Yields approximately ¾ cup [180 g]

½ cup [120 g] crème fraiche

¼ cup [60 ml] buttermilk

1 Tbsp chopped chives

1 Tbsp chopped fresh dill

1 tsp freshly squeezed lemon juice

¼ tsp garlic powder

¼ tsp salt, plus more for seasoning

⅛ tsp freshly ground black pepper, plus more for seasoning

In a small mixing bowl, whisk together all the ingredients. Taste and adjust the seasoning by adding more salt or pepper, if needed. Serve right away.

Crème Fraîche

NEW YEAR'S EVE MARTINI BAR

Looking to get fancy this New Year's Eve? I've got you covered with this martini bar, but you are on your own when it comes to picking out the perfect black dress, shade of red lipstick, or pocket square to complement your tie.

Styling Notes

Martinis are traditionally made individually rather than in a big-batch. Create a self-serve drink station by putting out a nice bottle of gin or vodka and vermouth along with a shaker, a cocktail jigger or small liquid measuring glass, serving stirrers or toothpicks, martini or coupe glasses, and a card with handwritten instructions on how to make a classic dry martini (with variation suggestions).

Make-Ahead Game Plan

Syrups can be made up to a week before and stored in airtight containers in the refrigerator. If making the Herby Brown Sugar Nuts (page 104), make those up to 2 days in advance and store in an airtight container at room temperature. Assemble the spread 30 minutes before guests arrive (minus the ice). Put out the ice right as guests are arriving.

Snack Pairing

The Herby Brown Sugar Nuts (page 104) go wonderfully with this spread. The sweet-and-savory nuts perfectly complement the bracing alcohol in the drink.

Spread Type

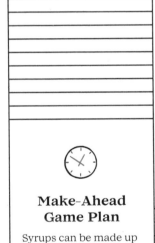

Drink Station

Flavor Combination Ideas

Skip the olive and add 1½ to 2 oz [45 to 60 ml] (depending on how sweet you like your cocktails) of the Cranberry-Orange Syrup or Lemon-Rosemary Syrup (page 280) to your classic gin martini.

Garnish with orange peels or rosemary.

Wyatt's Sidebar

Serve cocktail weenies with toothpicks to amplify the retro feel of the martinis.

Makes 20 drinks

(Feel free to scale this one up or down depending on how many people you are hosting.)

1 bottle of dry gin or vodka (you'll need 30 fl oz [900 ml])

1 bottle (or at least 10 fl oz [300 ml]) dry vermouth

1 batch Cranberry-Orange Syrup (page 280)

1 batch Lemon-Rosemary Syrup (page 280)

20 pieces various garnish options (such as green olives, lemon peels, orange peels, cranberries, rosemary sprigs, etc.)

Place the bottles of gin and vermouth on your drink station. Transfer the syrups to small serving pitchers and add them to the drink station. Place the garnish options in nice serving bowls and add them to the drink station.

Place ice in an ice bucket on the drink station right before guests arrive.

Classic
Dry Martini

Why mess with the classics if they are as good as a standard dry martini? Either gin or vodka will work with the recipe, depending on your preference.

Yields 1 drink

3 Tbsp dry gin or vodka

1 Tbsp dry vermouth

Green olive or lemon twist,
    for garnish

Pour the gin and vermouth in a cocktail shaker and fill the shaker with ice. Shake or stir, then strain into a martini glass. Garnish with an olive and/or lemon twist and serve.

Cranberry-Orange Syrup

This syrup is not only delicious but also creates the most beautiful and festive red hue for your cocktails!

Yields 2 cups [480 ml]

---

1 cup [200 g] sugar

1 cup [110 g] fresh or frozen cranberries

½ cup [120 ml] freshly squeezed orange juice (from 1 large orange)

In a medium saucepan over medium-high heat, combine 1 cup [240 ml] of water, the sugar, cranberries, and orange juice and bring to a boil. Immediately lower the heat to low and simmer, stirring often, until all the sugar has dissolved, about 3 minutes. Remove from the heat and let sit for 20 minutes. Strain the mixture through a fine-mesh sieve and discard any solids. Use the syrup right away or store it in the refrigerator in an airtight container for up to 1 week.

Lemon-Rosemary Syrup

I love this flavor combo, as the rosemary brings earthiness to the syrup while the lemon helps brighten it up.

Yields 1½ cups [360 ml]

---

1 cup [200 g] sugar

½ cup [120 ml] freshly squeezed lemon juice (from about 4 lemons)

2 sprigs rosemary

Zest of 1 lemon

In a medium saucepan over medium heat, combine 1 cup [240 ml] of water, the sugar, lemon juice, and rosemary and bring to a boil. Immediately lower the heat to low and simmer, stirring often, until all the sugar has dissolved, about 3 minutes. Remove from the heat, add the lemon zest, and let sit for 20 minutes. Strain the mixture through a fine-mesh sieve and discard any solids. Use the syrup right away or store it in the refrigerator in an airtight container for up to 1 week.

Cranberry-Orange Syrup

Acknowledgments

Thank you so much to Wyatt, my collaborator and husband, not only for always being down to contribute to my food projects but also for dealing with my frantic and busy self for the year (and then some) of the cookbook writing and photographing process. No one has as much patience as you!

Thank you to my agent, Cindy Uh, for always being my biggest advocate and going above and beyond throughout all the years we've worked together. None of this would be possible without your enthusiasm, negotiation skills, and constant support! I'm forever grateful for the time you've spent with me brainstorming, encouraging, and sharing wisdom.

Thank you so much to everyone at Chronicle Books, particularly Sarah Billingsley, Lizzie Vaughan, Cynthia Shannon, Joyce Lin, and Claire Gilhuly for believing in this project and bringing it to life in ways I could have never done on my own. And to Mali Fischer for the gorgeous illustrations that complement my words so perfectly!

Thank you so much to all of the recipe testers, friends, and family who helped make sure that these recipes not only work in my kitchen but also in kitchens all over the world: Barbara Brosher, Kathy Cherven, Jan Davis, Aly Fry, Hayden Fry, Geo Fry, George Fry, Kaleen Fry, Sarah El Hattab, Paige Lafuente, Stephanie 'Evs' Lebamoff, Leah Lukas, Megan MacDonald, Kacy Netherland, Erica Sagon, Susie Tanney, Kelsey Trost, Kurt, Lucy and Baby Kurt Westerhausen, Conchita M. Westerhausen, Curt Westerhausen, and Zeynep Yasar.

Thank you to Meg Alvarez and Dwell Vacations in Union Pier, Michigan, for allowing us to spend a few days at one of your gorgeous properties to photograph a large portion of this book. And thank you so much (again!) to Leah Lukas, my mom, and Wyatt for helping assist, prep, and style on those days at the property. I couldn't have done it without you all!

Thank you to the FAR Center for Contemporary Art in Bloomington, Indiana (with a special shout out to Abigail Gardner), for letting me photograph another portion of this book (during a pandemic, no less!) in their library studio space.

And finally, thank you so much to you for picking up, reading, and cooking through this cookbook. <3

Index